KT-418-893

FRANKENSTEIN
CHARACTER STUDIES

DAVID HIGGINS

NORWICH CITY COLLEGE LIBRARY		
Stock No.	217249	
Class	823.7 HIG	
Cat.	SSA	Proc. 3WL

continuum

Continuum

The Tower Building
11 York Road
London SE1 7NX

80 Maiden Lane, Suite 704
New York
NY 10038

www.continuumbooks.com

© David Higgins 2008

All rights reserved. No part of this publication may be reproduced or
transmitted in any form or by any means, electronic or mechanical,
including photocopying, recording, or any information storage or
retrieval system, without prior permission in writing from the
publishers.

David Higgins has asserted his right under the Copyright, Designs and
Patents Act, 1988, to be identified as Author of this work.

First published 2008

British Library Cataloguing-in-Publication Data
A catalogue record for this book is available from the British Library.

ISBN: 978-0-8264-9436-8 (hardback)
978-0-8264-9437-5 (paperback)

Library of Congress Cataloging-in-Publication Data
A catalog record for this book is available from the Library of
Congress.

Typeset by Servis Filmsetting Ltd, Manchester
Printed and bound in Great Britain by
MPG Books Ltd, Bodmin, Cornwall

FRANKENSTEIN

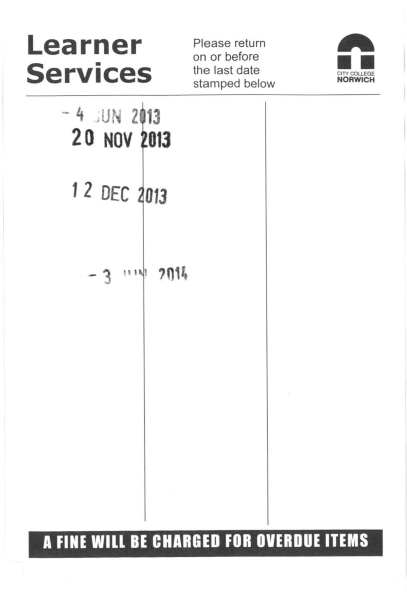

Learner Services

Please return on or before the last date stamped below

CITY COLLEGE
NORWICH

- 4 JUN 2013

20 NOV 2013

1 2 DEC 2013

- 3 JUN 2014

A FINE WILL BE CHARGED FOR OVERDUE ITEMS

217 249

CONTINUUM CHARACTER STUDIES

CONTENTS

SERIES EDITOR'S PREFACE

This series aims to promote sophisticated literary analysis through the concept of character. It demonstrates the necessity of linking character analysis to texts' themes, issues and ideas, and encourages students to embrace the complexity of literary characters and the texts in which they appear. The series thus fosters close critical reading and evidence-based discussion, as well as an engagement with historical context, and with literary criticism and theory.

Character Studies was prompted by a general concern in literature departments about students responding to literary characters as if they were real people rather than fictional creations, and writing about them as if they were two-dimensional entities existing in an ahistorical space. Some students tend to think it is enough to observe that King Lear goes 'mad', that Frankenstein is 'ambitious', or that Vladimir and Estragon are 'tender and cruel'. Their comments are correct, but obviously limited.

Thomas Docherty, in his *Reading (Absent) Character: Towards a Theory of Characterization in Fiction*, reminds us to relate characters to ideas but also stresses the necessity of engaging with the complexity of characters:

> If we proceed with the same theory as we apply to allegory [that a character represents one thing, such as Obstinate in Bunyan's *Pilgrim's Progress*], then we will be led to accept that Madame Bovary 'means' or 'represents' some one essence or value, however complex that essence may be. But perhaps, and

more likely, she is many things, and perhaps some of them lead to her character being incoherent, lacking unity, and so on. [. . .] It is clearly wrong to say, in a critical reading, that Kurtz, for example, in Conrad's *Heart of Darkness* represents evil, or ambition, or any other one thing, and to leave it at that; nor is Jude a representative of 'failed aspirations' in Hardy's *Jude the Obscure*; nor is Heathcliff a representation of the proletariat in Emily Brontë's *Wuthering Heights*, and so on. There may be elements of truth in some of these readings of character, but the theory which rests content with trying to discover the singular simple essence of character in this way is inadequate [. . .]. (1983, p. xii)

King Lear, for example, is complex, so not easily understandable, and is perhaps 'incoherent, lacking unity'; he is fictional, so must be treated as a construct; and he does not 'mean' or 'represent' one thing. We can relate him to ideas about power, control, judgement, value, sovereignty, the public and the private, sex and sexuality, the body, nature and nurture, appearance, inheritance, socialization, patriarchy, religion, will, blindness, sanity, violence, pessimism, hope, ageing, love, death, grief – and so on.

To ignore this, and to respond to Lear as if he is a real person talking ahistorically, means we simplify both the character and the play; it means, in short, that we forget our responsibilities as literary critics. When, for example, Lear cries, 'Howl, howl, howl, howl! O, you are men of stones!' (5.2.255), it would be wrong to ignore our emotional response, to marginalize our empathy for a father carrying his dead daughter, but we must also engage with such other elements as: the meaning and repetition of 'Howl' (three howls in some editions, four in others); the uncertainty about to whom 'you are men of stones' is directed; what 'men of stones' meant to Shakespeare's audience; the various ways in which the line can be said, and the various effects produced; how what Lear says relates to certain issues in the play and introduces new ideas about being human; what literary critics have written about the line; and what literary theorists have said, or might say, about it.

When we embrace the complexity of character, when we undertake detailed, sensitive critical analysis that acknowledges historical context, and literary criticism and theory, and when we relate characters to themes, issues and ideas, the texts we study blossom, beautifully and wonderfully, and we realize that we have so much more to say about them. We are also reminded of why they are worthy of study, of why they are important, of why they are great.

Ashley Chantler
University of Chester, UK

ACKNOWLEDGEMENTS

Anna Sandeman at Continuum commissioned this book and Colleen Coalter provided helpful editorial assistance. Ashley Chantler has proved an excellent editor, and, as always, his friendship and humour have been invaluable. I am grateful to all three, particularly for their understanding with regard to the late submission of the typescript. Friends and colleagues at the University of Leeds provided cheery encouragement during the writing process. Finally, I would like to thank the students at Chester, Leeds and York to whom I have taught *Frankenstein*: their ideas and enthusiasm have greatly enriched my enjoyment and understanding of the novel.

AN OVERVIEW OF *FRANKENSTEIN*

Writing on *Frankenstein* is a frightening experience. Over the last 30 years or so, the novel has generated an enormous amount of critical commentary, much of it concerned with placing it in the context of its time and tracing its wide range of literary and philosophical sources. Mary Shelley's novel, it is now apparent, was extraordinarily receptive to the intellectual culture of Romantic-period Europe. It can be difficult to work out how to write about it without getting lost in the wide range of texts and ideas that influenced and informed it, especially given that scholarship is constantly adding to this list. For example, *Frankenstein*'s treatment of the life sciences has been related to the writings and experiments of (among others) John Abernethy, Giovanni Aldini, Johann Friedrich Blumenbach, Erasmus Darwin, Humphry Davy, Franz Joseph Gall, Luigi Galvani, John Hunter, Johann Kaspar Lavater, William Lawrence, Lorenz Oken, Johann Wilhelm Ritter, and Georg Ernst Stahl. Such lists produce, in me at least, a degree of intellectual anxiety, a sense I might never know enough to be able to analyse the text with adequate authority and sophistication. Faced with such anxiety, the only way to proceed, whether writing a book or an undergraduate essay, is to go back to first principles; to ask the question, 'What is *my* interest in this text?', and to *use* criticism and scholarship in order to develop one's own personal response.

This book focuses on *Frankenstein*'s characters, and seeks to use analysis of those characters as a way into examining the novel's wider themes and concerns. In this introduction, and indeed throughout the book, I supply some background information in order to help you better to understand the novel, but I have tried to avoid getting bogged down in contextual matters. There is a great deal of enlightening critical work on *Frankenstein* and its contexts, and I refer to various secondary texts during my discussion; see also the Further Reading section. Rather like the Creature himself, Shelley's novel is something of a mishmash, made up of different texts and ideas that do not always fit together perfectly. However, this book also recognizes that for most readers it is much more than this. *Frankenstein* is a text to which we may have a strong emotional response, describing scenes and situations that may move and excite us, and containing characters whose motivations and moral worth we are likely to find interesting and ambiguous. To try to write literary criticism in terms of readerly emotion and sympathy can be intellectually unproductive; on the other hand, and especially given that this book is structured around the discussion of character and characterization, it is important to recognize that such responses exist and that they are not somehow illegitimate.

In order to start analysing character in *Frankenstein* we need to think about its genre: what sort of text is it? It is typically described as a Gothic novel, which was a popular genre in the late eighteenth and early nineteenth centuries. Gothic novels sought to produce fear and suspense in their readers: events often took place in a medieval setting (hence Gothic) such as an old castle, and their protagonists (often innocent young women) were faced with various dangers, secrets and supernatural phenomena. As Fred Botting has suggested, Gothic texts are concerned with apparent threats to civilized values, 'threats associated with supernatural and natural forces, imaginative excesses and delusions, religious and human evil, social transgression, mental disintegration and spiritual corruption' (1995b, p. 2). Although *Frankenstein* is set in the late 1790s rather than the medieval period, its engagement with all the themes listed above, and particularly its fascination with its obsessive protagonist's transgression of the boundary between life and death, make it an authentically Gothic text.

Gothic novels were often described in the Romantic period as 'romances'; that is, stories of fantasy and the improbable.[1] We need to be aware of this when thinking about character. *Romance* does not try to describe the psychological complexity that we associate with the *realist* fiction of a writer like George Eliot (1819–80). Characterization in Gothic fiction, while it can be detailed and evocative, tends to be driven by the demands of the plot, and often associates particular characters with fairly simple qualities that they display over time, rather than with complex psychologies that change and develop. It is difficult when analysing a novel not sometimes to discuss its characters as if they are 'real people'. But it is important to bear in mind that they are textual constructions, and furthermore that *Frankenstein* is a novel that may not always be particularly concerned with presenting its characters as 'real'. Matters are made more complicated by the novel's narrative structure: a set of 'framed' first-person narratives. We find out about Walton's character through his letters to his sister; we find out about Frankenstein's character through Walton's perspective; and we find out about the Creature's character through Walton's perspective on Frankenstein's perspective. We need to be aware, then, of the distance between us and the events described and not simply take, for example, Frankenstein's assessment of the Creature at face value. This distance is emphasized by the fact that these narratives are *retrospective*: events are described after they have happened, in some cases a long time after. In practice, of course, we have to take much of what the characters tell us on trust if we are to make any sense of the novel, but it is important that we remain aware that everything we read about is mediated through various perspectives.

It is sometimes claimed that *Frankenstein*, particularly in its first edition, is not very well written. Clearly some passages are awkward and/or overly complex, and certain words and phrases are arguably overused. The plot also has its loose ends and inconsistencies, as well as relying on some unlikely coincidences. In a recent newspaper article, Germaine Greer goes so far as to suggest that 'it is not a good, let alone a great novel and hardly merits the attention it has been given'.[2] *Frankenstein* does not need me to defend it, but in response it seems worth pointing out that for almost two centuries it has had enormous mythic power, and, furthermore, that many other important works in the literary canon

3

are not particularly convincingly plotted, or even well written. Also, the power of the myth should not distract us from the power of the text. Shelley's prose may not be perfect, but it is intellectually rich and can be powerfully emotive.[3] Even its repetitions add to its effect. *Frankenstein* is amenable to close reading and there is plenty of that in this book. In my experience, students sometimes become anxious about close textual engagement, particularly when it applies to prose. One question that often arises is, 'But did the author really mean that?' In response, I would say first that it is impossible to know what the author *really* meant, and, second, that it does not matter. For example, there is no way of knowing whether Mary Shelley intended (whatever that means) to make Frankenstein and the Creature call each other 'wretches' as a way of linking the two of them, and of suggesting to the reader that there might be important similarities between their situations. However, whatever her intention, this similarity of rhetoric has certain effects, and in my view it is the job of the critic to think about what those effects are.

This book has a simple structure. Given that *Frankenstein* is dominated by the perspectives of its three major characters, I have focused my discussion on them, and brought in the other characters (who are generally underdrawn) when appropriate. The first chapter analyses Robert Walton, the explorer who tells the whole story of the novel within a letter to his sister. The second focuses on Victor Frankenstein, considering in particular how Shelley uses him as a way of interrogating Romantic notions of masculine genius, as well as the close parallels and connections that develop between him and the Creature. It also discusses his family and his friend Henry Clerval. Chapter 3 examines the Creature's narrative, focusing on the way in which his character is *made* by his experiences, particularly those of his surrogate family, the De Laceys, and also on his relationship with Frankenstein. The Conclusion consolidates the work done by the chapters in terms of relating the novel's characterization to its wider concerns. The rest of this Introduction comprises short sections giving contextual information that seems to me to be important to a basic understanding of *Frankenstein*. This information is inevitably compressed and to some extent simplified;

4

more detailed accounts of all the areas discussed below can be found in works listed in the section on Further Reading.

BIOGRAPHY

Mary Wollstonecraft Shelley (*née* Godwin) was born on 30 August 1797, the daughter of William Godwin (1756–1836) and Mary Wollstonecraft (1759–97), two of the most notorious radical thinkers of the 1790s.[4] Wollstonecraft died eleven days later from an infection that she had contracted following the birth. Godwin single-handedly brought up Mary and her half-sister Fanny Imlay Godwin (1794–1817; she was the illegitimate daughter of Wollstonecraft from a previous relationship) until 1801, when he married a widow, Mary Jane Vial (1766–1841), who brought two more illegitimate children into the family. Mary Wollstonecraft Godwin, as she was then called, seems mainly to have been educated at home and proved to be a remarkably precocious and intellectually voracious child. Biographers and critics have frequently drawn attention to her complex relationship with her father (to whom *Frankenstein* is dedicated), a combination of hero worship and rebelliousness, and her dislike of his second wife. The death of her mother also greatly affected her. It is notable that maternal figures are almost entirely absent from *Frankenstein*: Walton does not mention his mother; Frankenstein's mother dies prematurely; the Creature has no mother; and there is no mother in the De Lacey family.[5]

In November 1812, when Mary was 15, she first met the 20-year-old poet Percy Bysshe Shelley (1792–1822; hereafter PBS) and his wife Harriet Westbrook (1795–1816). PBS was an acolyte and a financial supporter of Mary's father. During the following 18 months, Mary was away from London much of the time, staying at the home of William Baxter (another admirer of Godwin) in Scotland. In May 1814, however, she met PBS again in London. His marriage was already close to collapse and, over a series of meetings, he and Mary fell in love. On 28 July 1814, they eloped to France, accompanied by Mary's stepsister Claire Clairmont (1798–1879). This was, of course, a serious social transgression and excited widespread disapproval among family and friends. After travelling around the Continent, they returned to England in September 1814; the couple had run out of money and Mary was pregnant. On 22 February 1815, she gave birth to a daughter, Clara, who only survived for twelve days. As various critics have noted, this painful experience, and Shelley's anxieties about childbirth, influenced the content of *Frankenstein* (see, for example, Mellor 1989, p. 41). This is perhaps most apparent in the case of a dream that she had several weeks after Clara's death: 'Dream that my little baby came to life again – that it had only been cold & that we rubbed it by the fire & it lived – I awake & find no baby – I think about the little thing all day' (Shelley 1987, vol. 1, p. 70).

The death of PBS's grandfather in January 1815 provided him with a large settlement and an annual income of one thousand pounds, a considerable sum in the early nineteenth century. The couple moved to Windsor in August 1815, and in January 1816 Mary gave birth to a son, William. A few months later the family, again accompanied by Claire Clairmont, travelled to Switzerland, in part to visit Claire's lover, the poet Lord Byron (1788–1824). It was here, at the Villa Diodati by Lake Geneva, that Mary began writing *Frankenstein*. In October 1816, Mary's half sister Fanny committed suicide, and in November so did PBS's wife Harriet. Mary and PBS, who had returned to England in September, married on 30 December 1816. *Frankenstein* was completed during 1817 and published in January 1818 (see below for a fuller account of its composition and publication). Mary's life was drastically transformed in July 1822, when PBS drowned off the Italian coast. She lived until 1851 and never remarried, going on to write several novels, most notably *The Last Man* (1826), as well as a wide variety of other works. The section on Further Reading suggests some texts that give a full account of her life and writings.

POLITICS

Although Mary Shelley was born over eight years after the beginning of the French Revolution, she, like others of her generation, looked back on it as an enormously important world-historical event, and experienced its aftershock. Although the Revolution is popularly associated with the storming of the notorious political prison, the Bastille, on 14 July 1789, it was actually a very complex set of events and processes that could be said to have begun in 1788, when the French king Louis XVI was advised to convene the Estates-General (the French equivalent of Parliament, which consisted of representatives of the nobility, the clergy and the so-called third estate of commoners) for the first time since 1614 in order to reorganize the nation's taxes and stave off imminent bankruptcy. It could be said to have ended in 1799 when the successful general Napoleon Bonaparte became the country's 'First Consul' and, indeed, at the end of that year he issued a proclamation stating that the Revolution was over. Over the next fifteen years, Napoleon would dominate Europe as Emperor of an expansionist France, finally defeated by the allied powers of Britain and Prussia at the battle of Waterloo on 18 June 1815.

The Revolution began as a fairly moderate movement to limit the power of the monarchy and the aristocracy. It was welcomed by many British writers, who saw France as a despotic country which needed to be more like its neighbour across the Channel, where the powers of the monarch were supposedly limited by Parliament. Although by modern democratic standards Britain was a grotesquely hierarchical and oppressive society during this time, there was a great deal of patriotic rhetoric idealizing British 'liberty' and perhaps it is true that its society was more free than that of France. As the Revolution became increasingly radical and republican, various British writers emerged to criticize its principles. The most powerful of these was Edmund Burke, whose *Reflections on the Revolution in France* (1790) argued strongly for the importance of tradition and sentiment in the smooth functioning of human society, and attacked the French attempt to create a new order based on reason and 'abstract rights'. Burke predicted that this would lead to anarchy and bloodshed and his conservative position gained authority as the Revolution became increasingly violent, culminating in the Terror of 1793–94, when the revolutionary government under Robespierre executed thousands of people.

Those intellectuals, like Shelley's parents, who wished fundamentally to change British society tended to believe strongly in
the principles of the Revolution – social equality, republicanism,
reason and so on – much as they deplored its descent
into violence. The most influential radical writer was Thomas
Paine (1737–1809), who responded to Burke in his *Rights of Man*
(1791), arguing that all human beings had natural rights, which
included the right to decide how they should be governed. The
popular success of Paine, and the increasing activity of radical
organizations such as the London Corresponding Society, led to
a government campaign of repression and intimidation directed
against British writers and activists who they believed were
threatening the country from within. By the late 1790s, British
reformers were in disarray. Britain and France were at war more
or less constantly between 1793 and 1815 and this made it
difficult to criticize the British state without seeming unpatriotic.
However, by the time that *Frankenstein* came to be written, arguments about the need for political change in order to ensure individual liberty once more came to prominence, not just in Britain,
but across Europe.

Frankenstein has often been read in the context of revolutionary politics; an obvious interpretation given the radical ideas of
Shelley's parents and of her husband PBS. One of the first people
to respond to Burke was her mother, Mary Wollstonecraft, in
A Vindication of the Rights of Men (1790). She is much better
known, however, for *A Vindication of the Rights of Woman*
(1792), a foundational feminist text that argued that as women
were rational beings, society needed to rethink how they were
educated and allowed to behave. Wollstonecraft was not a feminist in the modern sense of the word, for ultimately she saw a
woman's primary duties to lie in motherhood and the home.
However, her emphasis on the importance of domestic affections
for men as well as women, and on the dangers of a disjunction
between male and female spheres, had a profound impact on
Frankenstein.

Shelley's father William Godwin responded to the French
Revolution and the ensuing political controversy in two books,
both of which influenced *Frankenstein*: his political treatise, the

Enquiry Concerning Political Justice, and Its Influence on Morals and Happiness (1793), and his novel *Caleb Williams* (1794). Godwin has been called the father of 'philosophical anarchism': the *Enquiry* proposes an ideal world in which there is no need for government because every human being behaves on rational principles. Godwin believed that through a gradual process of Enlightenment such a vision could be realized and human society could be 'perfected'. *Caleb Williams*, which has the alternative title of *Things as They Are*, tells the story of how the young protagonist Caleb finds out that his chivalrous and benevolent aristocratic master Falkland has murdered a vicious rival and allowed someone else to be convicted of the crime. Fearing Caleb will reveal the truth, Falkland frames him for theft, and he spends much of the novel on the run from the authorities. Eventually he wins out through his forbearance and honesty. In the figure of Falkland, Godwin produced a powerful critique of Burke's idealization of chivalry, and his depiction of power and surveillance evokes the counter-revolutionary climate of the mid-1790s. The way in which Caleb and Falkland wrestle with each other throughout the novel, swapping the roles of pursuer and pursued, foreshadows the relationship between Frankenstein and the Creature, and the injustice of Justine's execution echoes Caleb's travails at the hands of the legal system.

ROUSSEAU AND THE ROMANTIC SELF

I have until now deliberately avoided using the term 'Romanticism' in this Introduction because it is extraordinarily difficult to define, covering as it does such a broad set of cultural changes and concerns that affected Europe during the period from around 1780 to 1830. Its adjectival form, 'Romantic', is less contentious when simply used as a convenient way of referring to this period. However, a phrase such as 'the Romantic self' perhaps implies more than that. If one was to start making some tentative generalizations about Romanticism, one might first note the impact of revolutionary politics on European thought and culture during the late eighteenth and early nineteenth centuries. But a good second point would be to note the literary and artistic fascination with subjectivity and introspection: for example, the experience of the solitary self in nature. This is not to suggest that earlier historical periods were not interested in personal identity, but it does not seem to me to be going too far to suggest that in eighteenth-century European literature and thought, the self becomes increasingly defined by its inner life and 'authenticity', rather than by its relationship to others through kinship, descent, social status and so on. A key figure here is the Genevan thinker Jean-Jacques Rousseau (1712–78), whose writings inform *Frankenstein* in multiple and complex ways.

Rousseau wrote several works that had profound cultural impact. In the *Discours sur l'origine de l'inégalité [Discourse on the Origins of Inequality]* (1755), he attacked 'civilization' as leading to selfishness, deceit, and unhappiness, and suggested that human beings were, or could be, most fulfilled in a 'state of nature'. His sentimental epistolary novel *Julie, ou la nouvelle Héloïse [Julie, or the new Heloise]* (1761) was enormously popular. His educational tract, *Émile* (1762), was revolutionary in its emphasis on childhood *development*, but was attacked by Mary Wollstonecraft, among others, for its claim that women should be educated very differently from men due to their natural weakness and passivity. In *Du contrat social [The Social Contract]* (1762), he argued that all sovereignty lies in the 'general will' of the people: this sovereignty is exercised through government but may be revoked at any time. This theory had a powerful impact on European political thought, so much so that (wrongly) he was later to be blamed by conservative writers like Burke as the principal instigator of the French Revolution.

Due to the controversial political and religious aspects of his work, Rousseau was forced to flee from France in 1762 (where he had been living for some years) after his arrest was ordered by the French government. He was also censored by the Genevan authorities and renounced his citizenship in 1763. During his final years, marred by bitterness, paranoia, and controversy, he wrote some highly significant autobiographical writings, most notably the *Confessions* (1782–89) and the *Rêveries du promeneur solitaire [Reveries of the Solitary Walker]* (1782). These works were meant to defend him from his detractors and claimed to present an absolutely accurate picture of his true identity. However, the frankness of the *Confessions* gave his critics plenty of ammunition with which to attack him and the revolutionary ideology with which he became associated. For Edmund Burke, the gap between Rousseau's theoretical sympathy for humankind, and his actual behaviour in life, is typical of the hypocrisy of the French Revolutionaries:

It is that new invented virtue [. . .] that led their moral hero constantly to exhaust the stores of his powerful rhetorick in the expression of universal benevolence; whilst his heart was incapable of harbouring one spark of parental affection. (Burke 1999, pp. 512–13)

Here Burke is referring to the well-known fact, admitted by Rousseau himself, that he had given up five of his children to a foundling hospital. *Frankenstein* does not just engage with many of Rousseau's ideas but, in its depiction of the dangers of paternal neglect, with him personally as a historical figure (O'Rourke 1989).

Charles Taylor states that Rousseau 'is the starting point of a transformation in modern culture towards a deeper inwardness and a radical autonomy' (p. 363). For Rousseau, the individual self is, or at least should be, an autonomous source of meaning that is separate from culture. It does not, or at least should not, rely on the existence of others either for its existence or its attributes. On the one hand, we might see such individualism as progressive, encouraging a distrust of traditional social structures and the growth of democratic and republican movements that emphasize individual freedom. On the other, it might also seem defensive and negative, leading to withdrawal and self-obsession. *Frankenstein* registers both these aspects of Rousseau's thought. In Chapter 3, I consider the importance to the Creature's narrative of ideas from the *Discourse on Inequality* and *Émile*. But it seems worth noting here that the introspective rhetoric of Rousseau's later writings also influenced the novel. Consider, for example, the beginning of the *Rêveries*:

So now I am alone in the world, with no brother, neighbour or friend, nor any company left me but my own. The most sociable and loving of men has with one accord been cast out by all the rest. With all the ingenuity of hate they have sought out the cruellest torture for my sensitive soul, and have violently broken all the threads that bound me to them. I would have loved my fellow-men in spite of themselves. It was only by ceasing to be human that they could forfeit my affection. So now they are strangers and foreigners to me; they no longer exist for me, since such is their will. But I, detached as I am from them and from the whole world, what am I? This must now be the object of my inquiry. (Rousseau 1979b, p. 27)

Sounding rather like the Creature, and at times Frankenstein, Rousseau describes his utter solitude and separation from normal social bonds. Like the Creature, he sought the love and society of others, only to be repulsed. Now humanity ('*all* the rest') is monstrous (no longer 'human') and 'foreign' to him and, he claims, has disappeared from his consciousness All that is left is for him to turn inward and, like the Creature, enquire into his own being: 'what am I?'. Yet this sort of confessional writing is actually anything but self-enclosed, for it seeks to construct a relationship with a reader who is imagined to provide the sympathetic bond that the speaker lacks. Similarly, the 'confessions' of Walton, Frankenstein and the Creature, while seemingly concerned only with the suffering, alienated self, show a continued desire to connect with others, even if such a connection proves elusive.

SCIENCE

The scientific context of *Frankenstein* has been so much discussed in recent years that any short summary is bound to be inadequate; see the section on Further Reading for more detailed work. The two most important (and related) scientific contexts lie in physics and physiology. Electricity was a mysterious and exciting 'fluid' in eighteenth-century culture, producing numerous dramatic public experiments, perhaps most notably those by

Humphry Davy (1778–1829) at the Royal Institution. Luigi Galvani (1737–98) famously made a frog's legs twitch through the application of electricity, inventing the science of galvanism. In 1802–03 his nephew Giovanni Aldini (1762–1834) visited London to promote and defend his uncle's work. In one infamous experiment, he applied electricity to the heads of executed criminals, causing the muscles to contract and their facial expressions to change.

A number of natural scientists, such as the influential Erasmus Darwin (1731–1802), made links between electricity and the idea of the 'life force' (Shelley 1999, pp. 20–21). Crucial is the vitalist debate between John Abernethy (1764–1831) and his former pupil William Lawrence (1783–1867), who was a friend of PBS. Abernethy argued that life was a 'superadded' substance on to matter, akin to electricity or magnetism, a sort of invisible fluid. This was an orthodox position in religious terms, suggesting that God implanted life into matter. Lawrence, on the other hand, was a materialist, arguing that life came from the body, the sum of its parts, and mocking Abernethy's idea about an added fluid. He was criticized by some conservative critics as questioning the existence of the soul. Where Shelley's novel stands in terms of this debate is rather unclear: that Frankenstein succeeds in vitalizing dead matter would suggest its support for Abernethy's principles, although Marilyn Butler argues that they are actually being satirized (Shelley 1998, pp. xx–xxi).[6]

COMPOSITION, PUBLISHING AND RECEPTION HISTORY

Shelley was 18 years old when she began writing *Frankenstein* in June 1816. The story of its composition was first told by the author herself in her introduction to the third edition of 1831 (Shelley 1998, pp. 192–97). It began, apparently, with a ghost story competition between Byron, his doctor John William Polidori (1795–1821), PBS, and Shelley when they were staying at Byron's villa in Switzerland.[7] During the same period, Shelley states that she 'was a devout but nearly silent listener' to various conversations between Byron and PBS, including one concerning 'the nature of the principle of life' (Shelley 1998, p. 195). Various recent scientific experiments were discussed, including the reanimation of a corpse through galvanism. Shelley describes this as leading to a powerful nightmare:

> I saw the pale student of unhallowed arts kneeling beside the thing he had put together. I saw the hideous phantasm of a man stretched out, and then, on the working of some powerful engine, show signs of life, and stir with an uneasy, half-vital motion. Frightful must it be; for supremely frightful would be the effect of any human endeavour to mock the stupendous mechanism of the Creator of the world.

The 'pale student' flees, hoping that the 'thing' will 'subside into dead matter'. He eventually sleeps but on waking, 'the horrid thing stands at his bedside, opening his curtains and looking on him with yellow, watery, but speculative eye' (Shelley 1998, p. 196).

Shelley's nightmare does not have to be taken at face value; placing the inspiration for the novel in a dream may have been a way of reducing her own responsibility for its disturbing content. Her account of *Frankenstein*'s origins has also been read as typifying the polite self-effacement that was expected of women writers in the nineteenth century, suggesting as it does that somehow the thoughts of Byron and PBS were working through her. Furthermore, as Butler notes (Shelley 1998, p. 260), Shelley's mention of the 'Creator of the world' here suggests how the 1831 edition gives greater emphasis to the creation of the Creature as a *religious* transgression than does the original version of the novel. However, some aspects of the dream do shed light on the original version. Her description of the Creature as 'the hideous phantasm of a man' is worth considering because of the multiple meanings of 'phantasm'. First, the Creature is represented as a sort of hallucination, existing in her mind as the dreamer of the dream and the author of the novel, but also in the mind of Victor Frankenstein, who is the 'author' of the Creature's existence. Secondly, the phrase suggests that the Creature is a poor copy, a parody, of a human being. And thirdly, the fact that there is something ghostly (phantasmal) about its presence suggest that the roots of its existence lie in death and decay. This passage, therefore, to some extent carries out the 'Othering' of the Creature – the representation of him as an inhuman 'thing' – that is characteristic of attitudes to him throughout *Frankenstein*. However, Shelley's novel, of course, problematizes this 'Othering' by giving the Creature a voice, and the fact that it is actually much more than a 'horrid thing' is suggested by the final words of the quotation. The Creature's eye is speculative not only because it is watching 'the pale student' (the Latin word *speculari* means to spy out or to watch) but also because it has the power to think for itself (to speculate); to use reason (supposedly a human attribute) to make sense of its experiences and therefore of the world.

Shelley worked on her story in June and July 1816, and in August PBS seems to have encouraged her to expand it (Shelley 1996a, p. xciii). She continued writing during the autumn and winter, with corrections and transcription taking place in April and May 1817. It is clear that PBS was involved in some of the changes to the text, although the extent and importance of his involvement in the novel's composition is subject to critical debate (Leader 1996, pp. 167–205; Mellor 1989, pp. 57–69, 219–24; Shelley 1996c, pp. lxvi–lxxi).[8] The novel was sold to the publisher James Lackington in September and published (with a print run of five hundred) on 1 January 1818, along with a dedication to Shelley's father, William Godwin, and an unsigned Preface by PBS, writing in the character of the author. Several of *Frankenstein*'s early reviewers assumed that the novel was by PBS.[9]

Shelley's creation of a modern myth, as several critics have shown, had a powerful impact on nineteenth-century culture (Baldick 1990). It also, of course, became part of twentieth-century popular culture, due mainly to various cinematic adaptations (listed and discussed in Morton 2002, pp. 64–78). Allusion to *Frankenstein* is often used as a convenient shorthand for anyone wishing to express their concerns about the dangers of scientific advancement, although the extent to which this actually reflects the focus of the original novel is questionable. Regardless of *Frankenstein*'s influence on popular culture, it was probably not until the early 1970s that academic critics and scholars generally began to take it seriously; before then, its popular status meant that it was rarely considered to be worthy of study. Since then the amount of criticism on the novel has increased exponentially, and now includes a vast range of different approaches. Much important work has been done by feminist critics, who have tended to present it as a critique of masculine Romanticism and as a reflection of Shelley's own anxieties about childbirth and sexuality. Post-structuralist and psychoanalytical approaches to the novel have used the writings of Sigmund Freud, Jacques Lacan, and Jacques Derrida (among others) to analyse its representation of dreams, desire, and language (signification). In the last fifteen years or so, cultural critics and so-called New Historicists have done a great deal to reposition the text within early nineteenth-century scientific discourse. Important readings have also focused on the figure of the Creature as 'Other': Marxist critics have seen him as representing the oppressed proletariat (workers), whereas, more recently, he has been discussed in terms of imperialism and ideas of racial difference. Johanna M. Smith provides a useful essay on *Frankenstein*'s critical history in her edition of the novel, which also contains various critical extracts (Shelley 2000, pp. 237–61).

Two different versions of *Frankenstein* are widely available in modern editions: the original text of 1818, and the revised third edition of 1831. (The second edition of 1823 is very similar, although not identical, to the first.) Although Shelley made a number of stylistic improvements to the original text when preparing the third edition, I agree with those critics who have argued that the original is more coherent, more radical, and more interesting (see, for example, Anne K. Mellor's essay 'Choosing a Text of *Frankenstein* to Teach', in Behrendt 1990, pp. 31–37). Therefore I have decided to focus my discussion on the 1818 text: unless otherwise noted, references to the novel are to Marilyn Butler's Oxford World's Classics edition, entitled *Frankenstein or The Modern Prometheus (The 1818 Text)* (1998). In a useful appendix to this edition, Butler summarizes and lists the substantive changes that Shelley made to the 1831 version.[10] Given that, as Butler notes, there are changes to the characters of

Clerval, Frankenstein and Walton, I have provided a short appendix to this book analysing characterization in the third edition.

One last thing: in writing this book, I have found myself using more 'hedging' terms ('perhaps', 'might', 'may', and so on) than I think would normally be advisable in academic writing. Given that I find myself frequently crossing out such words when marking student essays, I think they need some justification. This lies in the nature of the book, which is meant to open up areas for thought and discussion, rather than to come up with arguments that close them off. The purpose of a term such as 'might' is to make you, as the reader, an active participant in the critical process. The job of this book is *not* to tell you what to think about *Frankenstein* and its characters, but to help you in developing your own response to the novel. Such a response needs to be supported and developed through textual evidence and critical awareness, of course, but it is only through personal engagement with a text that one will write on it with *vitality*, and produce work that is more than the sum of its parts.

CHAPTER 1

WALTON THE EXPLORER

WALTON'S BACKGROUND AND CHARACTER

Robert Walton's four letters to his sister, Margaret Saville, not only begin *Frankenstein* but also frame the stories told by Frankenstein and the Creature. In effect, therefore, the whole novel (mostly contained in the enormously long and seemingly unfinished fourth letter) is told from Walton's perspective, and thus an understanding of his character is vital for an understanding of the text. We discover a great deal about him in the opening pages. He is 28 years old and 'self-educated', having had no formal schooling (p. 9). It is implied that he has been brought up by his uncle Thomas, following the death of his father (p. 6): whether or not his father died before he was born is unclear, and we do not hear anything at all about his mother. Given that he is writing to his sister, his uncle may now also be dead. This is further suggested by the close affection that he seems to have for his 'dear, excellent' Margaret (p. 8).

As a child, Walton's only reading matter came from Thomas's library, which consisted entirely of accounts of 'all the voyages made for purposes of discovery' (p. 6). This might suggest that Thomas was or had been a mariner, as might the 'dying injunction' of his father forbidding Thomas to allow Walton 'to embark in a sea-faring life' (p. 6).[1] Walton's transgression of this injunction, and the apparent absence of a maternal presence in his childhood, prefigures Frankenstein's situation. The scientist's mother dies during his adolescence (p. 26) and he withdraws himself from and neglects his family when conducting the experiments leading to the creation of the Creature. This act, of course, has terrible consequences for the Frankensteins.

At the age of 14, Walton began reading poetry, which had a powerful effect on him. Using language typical of the Romantic celebration of the poetic imagination, he describes how poetry 'entranced my soul, and lifted it to heaven' (p. 6). We might describe this as a *sublime* experience: the passive soul is moved into a spiritual realm by an exterior force. Walton began to write poetry, and spent a year imagining that he might be recognized as a great genius by future generations; as he puts it, 'obtain a niche in the temple where the names of Homer and Shakespeare are consecrated' (p. 7). Romantic writers often used this sort of religious language to describe artistic endeavour – for Walton, the names of the two greatest European poets have been made *holy* by posterity – suggesting that the creation of art and poetry was a profoundly spiritual process. In its extreme form, this sort of language suggested that the individual genius had godlike powers of creativity. Various critics, perhaps most notably Paul A. Cantor, have shown that Mary Shelley is interrogating this idea in *Frankenstein*. Certainly, this brief passage from Walton's life history emphasizes his links to Frankenstein: both have powerful imaginations and are dreamers – Walton's 'day dreams' are 'fervent and vivid' (p. 4) and 'magnificent' (p. 9) – and both strongly desire the recognition of posterity.

Walton alludes to his 'failure' as a poet, although precisely what this means is unclear, and his inheritance of his cousin's fortune. At the age of 22, he resolved to voyage to the North Pole, and began training his body and mind to achieving this goal (p. 7). Like Frankenstein, Walton is a driven man, avoiding a life of 'ease and luxury' in pursuit of the 'glory' that would come from a successful expedition (p. 7). As well as this desire for acclaim, he is also driven by 'ardent curiosity' to see 'a part of the world never before visited' (p. 6). 'Ardent' is an interesting choice of adjective and, as we shall see in the next chapter, one frequently applied by Frankenstein to his own scientific explorations. Its original meaning in English is 'burning' or 'fiery' (the Latin word *ardere* means 'to burn'), but it has come to be used figuratively to mean 'glowing with passion, animated by keen desire, intensely eager' (*OED*). It suggests, then, the passionate intensity of Walton's desire to reach the North Pole. 'Ardour' is also a term sometimes associated with sexual love, and we might consider that both Walton and Frankenstein are isolated and loveless when they are engaged in their exploratory endeavours. Perhaps their obsessive attempts to pursue 'nature to her hiding places' (p. 36) are so peculiarly intense due to a sublimation (i.e. a diversion of the energy) of sexual desire.

In the opening letter, Walton writes of the great benefits that might be produced by discoveries made on his voyage, and states that 'I feel my heart glow with an enthusiasm which elevates me to heaven' (p. 6); here exploration has replaced poetry as the source of sublime elevation. The metaphor of the glowing heart links to his earlier use of 'ardent'. 'Enthusiasm' is another important word, and one also used by Frankenstein. Although in twenty-first-century English, 'enthusiasm' tends simply to mean 'strong interest' or 'eagerness', in the Romantic period it was a much more powerful, complex and ambivalent term. Its original meaning, obsolete by the time Shelley was writing, was 'possession by a God, supernatural inspiration' (*OED*). Walton is not using this meaning directly, but it clearly resonates with the reference to 'heaven', and it is important to bear in mind given that Frankenstein desires to emulate God by creating life from lifeless matter. In the eighteenth century, 'enthusiasm' was often used to refer to 'ill-regulated or misdirected religious emotion' (*OED*); for example, Methodism, which emphasizes a personal, emotional relationship with God, could be branded as 'enthusiasm'. The term was also sometimes used by conservative writers to attack political radicals, such as those who supported the French Revolution in the 1790s. However, as Iain McCalman states, 'it was also reworked and secularized by Romantic poets to signify the sublime inward inspiration necessary for true poetry' (p. 498).[2] That is, it was no longer necessarily a *religious* term, but maintained its spiritual overtones. Thus Walton is using 'enthusiasm' to refer to a mixture of excitement, passion and inspiration. Given its potentially negative connotations, though, it may be a signal for readers to consider the extent to which his eagerness to pursue his dreams might be foolish, dangerous, and excessive; and the explorer himself admits that his mind lacks 'regulation' (p. 9).

A constant theme in Walton's letters is his loneliness, which we need to bear in mind when judging his enthusiastic response to Frankenstein. He writes admiringly of the lieutenant and the ship's master (p. 9), but there is nobody on board with whom he has a close relationship. Despite asserting his good spirits, he wants 'an encouraging voice' to support him (p. 7):

> I have no friend, Margaret: when I am glowing with the enthusiasm of success, there will be none to participate my joy; if I am assailed by disappointment, no one will endeavour to sustain me in dejection. [. . .] I desire the company of a man who could sympathize with me; whose eyes would *reply* to mine. [. . .] I have no one near me, gentle yet courageous, possessed of a cultivated as well as of a capacious mind, whose tastes are like my own, to approve or amend my plans. How would such a friend repair the faults of your poor brother! I am too ardent in execution, and too impatient of difficulties. [. . .] I greatly need a friend who would have sense enough not to despise me as romantic, and affection enough for me to endeavour to regulate my mind. (pp. 8–9; my italics)

The key word here is 'sympathize'. Walton desires a friend who would be able to share and comprehend his emotions and enthusiasms. In the absence of his sister, from whom (as far as we know) he has not received any letters while in Russia, he seeks someone able to '*reply*' to him. Such a person would need to have a similar personality and aspirations, and would not look down on him as overly 'romantic' (dreamy, enthusiastic, sentimental); and yet, at the same time, he wants someone who would give helpful criticism, help him with the expedition, and, more generally, to 'regulate' his mind. We might think there is something rather selfish and narcissistic about this passage in its emphasis on the way in which this 'friend', a sort of better version of himself, would help to sustain him by sympathizing with Walton's feelings. Walton's loneliness and desire for human sympathy is similar to that of Frankenstein, who exiles himself from normal society by his actions, and to the Creature, who is exiled by society due to his grotesque appearance. Walton believes that in Frankenstein he has found the friend he seeks (p. 15); we might ask, though, whether Frankenstein is likely to 'repair' Walton's faults, or to worsen them.

CONTEXTS

Given that Walton is exploring the Arctic Sea when he encounters Frankenstein, *Frankenstein* can be read as a fictional travel narrative (or, perhaps, as a set of interlocking travel narratives told by Walton, Frankenstein, the Creature, and the De Lacey family). Travel writing was a popular genre in Britain during the Romantic period, as tourists, explorers and colonialists travelled through or settled in parts of the world which were sometimes virtually unknown to most British readers. Shelley had herself published *History of a Six Weeks' Tour* in 1817, describing her journey through Europe after eloping with PBS in 1814, and in using Walton she cleverly recognizes the public's appetite for stories of travel, adventure and exploration, particularly those describing strange and exotic locations.[3] Exploration was by no means a self-contained or politically neutral activity. It was strongly linked to scientific endeavour and discovery, and served to enable the expansion and entrenchment of the British Empire, which, having lost the American Colonies during the 1770s, became increasingly focused on Asia and the Pacific during the Romantic period.

To fully understand Walton's character, and his importance to the novel, we need to understand why he wants to get to the North Pole. He is uncharacteristic of Romantic-period polar explorers in that he believes that he is searching for a paradise, 'the region of beauty and delight [. . .] surpassing in wonders and in beauty every other region hitherto discovered on the habitable globe', where 'the sun is for ever visible [. . .] diffusing a perpetual splendour' (p. 5). This fantasy seems to come from his earlier poetical interests, deriving from classical authors and, significantly, John Milton's epic poem *Paradise Lost* (1667), a text which (as we shall see) has an important role in *Frankenstein* (Beck 2000). However, as Jessica Richard has pointed out, polar explorers in the late eighteenth and early nineteenth centuries, while not as fantastical in their imaginings as Walton, did believe in the 'romance' of 'an open, navigable sea over the North Pole' (p. 296), and this is also one of Walton's goals.[4]

We have already seen that he is driven by curiosity and a desire for personal glory. Like Frankenstein, his motives seem to be mixed, both selfish and altruistic. In the opening letter to his sister, he emphasizes the *public* good that may come from achieving his goal:

> I may there discover the wondrous power which attracts the needle; and may regulate a thousand celestial observations, that require only this voyage to render their seeming eccentricities consistent for ever. [. . .] [Y]ou cannot contest the inestimable benefit which I shall confer to all mankind to the last generation, by discovering a passage near the pole to those countries, to reach which at present so many months are requisite; or by ascertaining the secret of the magnet. (p. 6)

His journey, then, has two aims: first, to search for a sea passage near the North Pole, which would allow ships to travel from the Arctic Ocean (north of Russia) to 'the North Pacific Ocean'; and, secondly, to find out how magnetism ('the wondrous power which attracts the [compass] needle') works, presumably by discovering the North Magnetic Pole. Walton, using typically hyperbolical language, suggests that each of these discoveries would benefit humanity for as long as the species survives ('to the last generation').

Why does he believe these discoveries to be so important? The late eighteenth and early nineteenth century saw various British expeditions that sought to discover a passage through the North Pole. The main impetus for these expeditions was commercial and imperialistic: such a passage would allow trading vessels quicker and easier access to Asian countries, principally China and India, than was allowed by the current route around the tip of Africa. Commerce with these countries was enormously important to Britain's imperial power, and, of course, British control of India expanded during the nineteenth century. Much like modern-day proponents of globalization, Walton seems to assume that the increase in global trade encouraged by such a route would benefit the whole world. It might be argued, though, that he is unjustifiably conflating Britain's national interest with the interests of the whole of humanity: the discovery of a sea route through the polar ice was seen as important ultimately because it would give Britain an advantage over its European imperial competitors by allowing its merchants quicker and easier access to their Asian markets.

Walton's other goal introduces the theme of scientific discovery which is so crucial to the whole novel. There was strong scientific interest in magnetism during the Romantic period, not least because it was hoped that a full understanding of the phenomenon would help navigators (and therefore exploration and imperial expansion) by explaining and correcting compass variation: that is, the fact that there is divergence between the geographical north and the direction of a compass needle, which varies depending on where you are on the planet.[5] Walton hopes that by discovering the source of magnetism, he may help to 'regulate a thousand celestial observations'. It is not clear precisely what Shelley is alluding to here, but it may be that Walton believes that by understanding how magnetism works, navigation by the stars and navigation by compass could be reconciled, to the benefit of (British) mariners. Marilyn Butler notes that both magnetism and electricity were seen in the period as mysterious, invisible 'fluids' that 'surrounding individual bodies and the planets, were connected with heat and light, and might therefore be an essentially material source and condition of life' (p. 253); thus there are strong parallels between Walton's goals and Frankenstein's.[6] It may well be the case that 'Mary Shelley included terrestrial magnetism in what Anne Mellor has described as her "feminist critique of science" in which the male scientist is shown to desire to dominate and control a female nature' (Fulford *et al.* 2004, pp. 170–71). I will discuss the relationship between gender and science in more detail in the following chapter.

WALTON AND FRANKENSTEIN

One effect of the narrative frame is that, through Walton, we get an external view of Frankenstein before we hear his story. It also means that Frankenstein's story is told retrospectively, and that we start it having already seen how the events to be described have affected and damaged him. It is important, however, that we bear in mind that Walton's view is subjective and very much conditioned by his circumstances. Given his loneliness and desire for a sympathetic companion, it is not surprising that he is immediately fascinated by the mysterious traveller, whom he soon begins to love 'as a brother' (p. 15):

> I never saw a more interesting creature: his eyes have generally an expression of wildness, and even madness; but there are moments when, if any one performs an act of kindness towards him, or does him any the most trifling service, his whole countenance is lighted up, as it were, with a beam of benevolence and sweetness that I never saw equalled. But he is generally melancholy and despairing. (p. 14)

This emphasizes Frankenstein's suffering, misery, and 'wildness', which will later be explained by the experiences he has undergone, but also his innate and exceptional 'benevolence' (that is, his goodwill to other people). As Walton goes on to state, 'he must have been a noble creature in his better days, being even now in wreck so attractive and amiable' (p. 15). Again, 'amiable' emphasizes that Frankenstein cares about others, and serves to counterbalance the obsessive, driven, selfish character that we see in other parts of the novel. The metaphor 'in wreck' suggests not only that Frankenstein's ambitions and life have been destroyed, but links him further to Walton, whose ship is in literal danger of being wrecked on the Arctic ice (p. 12). It also links him to the Creature, who is frequently described as a 'wretch' (the two words have a similar etymology): both have lost the potential they once had and have become objects of pity. I discuss 'wretch' and its relevance to Walton, Frankenstein, and the Creature in more detail in the next chapter.

I am not suggesting that Frankenstein does not have the good qualities – benevolence, nobility, gentleness, wisdom, cultivation and eloquence (p. 15) – about which Walton is so effusive. But it is interesting that the novel places such emphasis on the explorer's loneliness, dreaminess and tendency to hyperbole; this may suggest to us that he is likely to idealize Frankenstein and to overlook his failings. Frankenstein, for Walton, is above all a romantic dreamer who, despite the hardship and danger of the Arctic environment, revels in its beauty:

> The starry sky, the sea, and every sight afforded by these wonderful regions, seems still to have the power of elevating his soul from earth. [. . .] [H]e may suffer misery, and be overwhelmed by disappointments; yet when he has retired into himself, he will be like a celestial spirit, that has a halo around him, within whose circle no *grief* or *folly* enters. (p. 16; my italics)

Thus Walton thinks of Frankenstein as very much like himself: a man whose imagination allows him to escape from earthly realities. The use of religious language ('soul', 'celestial spirit', 'halo') is important here, as it is when he asks his sister, with some embarrassment, 'Will you laugh at the enthusiasm I express concerning this *divine* wanderer?' (my italics; p. 17). The effect of all this is to present Frankenstein as a genius: someone who is more sensitive and spiritual than normal people. Someone who is closer to God. On a first reading of the novel, we might simply take Walton's claims at face value, but given the fact that Frankenstein's attempt to penetrate the mysteries of nature and to create life ends so disastrously, we might want to approach this religious language with a degree of suspicion. That is, it may say more about Walton's and Frankenstein's fantasies, enthusiasms, and arrogance than it does about their genius and spirituality, especially given the enormous amount of '*grief*' that Frankenstein's '*folly*' causes to those close to him.

When preparing to tell Walton his story, Frankenstein does not go as far as to suggest that it is a moral lesson for the explorer. However, he does note that it is possible that Walton's undertaking may prove to be 'a serpent to sting you', and suggests that listening to the story will be 'useful' to him, and 'enlarge' his 'faculties and understanding' (p. 17). Later on, he gives a much more explicit warning: 'learn from me [. . .] how dangerous is the acquirement of knowledge, and how much happier that man is who believes his native town to be the world, than he who aspires to become greater than his nature will allow' (p. 35). This begs the question as to how Walton reacts to the story in the final pages of the novel. Unsurprisingly, he is fascinated and excited by it, and believes it completely, partly because Frankenstein is so convincing, but also because he has seen the Creature before meeting the scientist, and he has also seen the letters between Felix and Safie (p. 178). But has he actually learned anything from it? Betty T. Bennett suggests that, as a result of Frankenstein's tale, Walton 'changes, placing the wishes of the community (the sailors on the ship) above his own ambitions' (Shelley 1996a, p. xxviii). I am not sure that things are so simple. Walton's ship is imprisoned by ice floes that threaten to destroy it and its crew, many of whom have already perished from the cold (p. 182). When some of the surviving sailors make the reasonable request that, should the ship get free of the ice, they return southward, Walton resists agreeing to this and tries to convince them to reconsider their demands. In this he is encouraged by Frankenstein's rousing speech to the crew, which I will discuss in the following chapter. Walton is clearly torn at this stage, stating that he would not lead his men 'further north, if they strenuously desired the contrary', but also that 'I had rather die, then return shamefully,– my purpose unfulfilled' (p. 183). Two days later, he agrees to turn back, blaming the crew for their 'cowardice and indecision', even though they have already shown great courage and suffered severe hardship. When the ice eventually clears, Walton tells Frankenstein that 'I cannot withstand their demands. I cannot lead them unwillingly to danger, and I must return' (p. 184). This does not seem to me to be evidence that Walton's outlook has fundamentally changed, but rather a simple statement of the facts. Faced with a mutinous crew, he has no other option than to turn back: they will not go north under his command and it is impossible for him to proceed without a ship. The pejorative language that he uses to describe the sailors, and his continued emphasis on 'glory' (p. 184), suggests that he does not believe that his continual enthusiasm for the expedition is reckless or misplaced. He has, in truth, learnt absolutely nothing from Frankenstein's story of the dangers of obsessional exploration that he believes might be applied to his own endeavour.

One might argue that the principal thing that Walton does learn from Frankenstein is to hate and despise the Creature, emphasizing his 'hideousness' (p. 187) and, like Frankenstein, referring to him as a 'fiend' and a 'wretch' (p. 188). Perhaps this is understandable, given Frankenstein's attractiveness as a character, Walton's sorrow at his death, and the Creature's grotesqueness, which causes such visceral reactions in every human being he encounters. Walton does not immediately seek to destroy the Creature (as Frankenstein has requested) but listens to him with 'a mixture of curiosity and compassion' (p. 187), as well as 'indignation' (p. 188). However, his binary categorization of Frankenstein as 'victim' and the Creature as 'villain', and the fact that Walton at no point acknowledges that Frankenstein's aspirations and actions may have been foolish or excessive, suggests, perhaps, that his perspective is flawed and limited.

CONCLUSION: THE FRAME NARRATIVE

Walton's own literary aspirations, and self-consciousness with which he describes recording Frankenstein's story and Frankenstein's amendments (pp. 18, 179), draw the reader's attention to issues of writing, reading and interpretation that resonate throughout *Frankenstein*.[7] As Mary Favret states, the novel confronts us with 'questions of narrative authority [. . .]. We wonder just whose story we are hearing' (p. 179).[8] One might add that we also wonder whose story has the most weight. As readers, we are presented with a range of interlocking narratives and interpretations and it is up to us to judge on the relationship between them and their relative importance in the economy of the novel as a whole. Furthermore, as Peter Brooks has noted, 'storytelling in *Frankenstein* is far from an innocent act: narratives have designs on their narratees that must be unravelled'

(Botting 1995a, p. 82). Walton's frame narrative is not a disinterested one. However, this may actually be helpful to us as readers for, by thinking about Walton's point of view, we gain our own perspective on Frankenstein's story and the theme of scientific exploration. This perspective is enabled mainly by various parallels between the two characters: they both lack a maternal presence as adults; they are both separated from family and friends; they are both strongly motivated by the desire for 'glory'; they are both 'enthusiasts' and dreamers; they are both fascinated by exploring areas that have not previously been explored; they both desire to discover the 'secrets' of nature and 'to penetrate ground that seems unredeemably dead, searching for a core of vital warmth unseen before' (Levine and Knoepflmacher 1979, p. 59).[9] Most significantly, both men seem unwilling or unable to consider the negative effects that their explorations may have on others. What we make of Walton, therefore, inevitably affects our judgement of Frankenstein, and our view of what the novel has to say about science, exploration, the imagination and masculinity.

CHAPTER 2

FRANKENSTEIN THE SCIENTIST

Frankenstein is often read as a parable of the dangers of uncontrolled scientific exploration, and Victor Frankenstein seen as the
archetype of the scientist who sacrifices all other considerations in
his quest for knowledge and power. This is a powerful reading of
the novel but perhaps a questionable one; even to use the word 'scientist' is anachronistic, for it was first coined in 1834, 16 years after
Frankenstein was originally published (*OED*). It would be more
historically accurate to describe him as a 'man of science' or a
'natural philosopher'. The set of interlinked discourses and cultural practices that we call 'science' were much more fluid and per-
meable in the early nineteenth century than in the present day, and
included methodologies and approaches that would now be considered profoundly unscientific. Having said that, the coining
of 'scientist' in the 1830s suggests the extent to which science
was becoming increasingly authoritative, 'acquiring institutional
and professional status', and 'recognisable as a distinct and coherent body of knowledge and practice' (Fulford *et al.*, p. 5). Shelley's
characterization of Frankenstein is partly informed by the
increasing profile and cultural entrenchment of science, and, given
modern anxieties about nuclear proliferation, global warming,
genetic modification and so on, it is hardly surprising that the
novel is often read as a straightforward critique of scientific aspirations.[1] However, such a reading is overly simplistic and ignores
the novel's ambiguities and inconsistencies, partly with regard to
Frankenstein's character: these reflect an area of human endeavour that, then as now, was confusing and mysterious, producing

excitement about its potential to improve human existence, along-side anxiety about its potential to cause harm.

FAMILY BACKGROUND, CHILDHOOD AND EARLY EDUCATION

Victor Frankenstein is born into one of the elite governing families of the republican city state of Geneva (p. 18).[2] His childhood is idyllic: 'No creature could have more tender parents than mine. My improvement and health were their constant care' (p. 19). The term 'creature' here, rather than 'child' or 'infant', serves to link Frankenstein and the Creature as *created* beings, and emphasizes the contrast between the 'care' of his parents and the complete lack of care he shows the Creature. When Frankenstein is four, his cousin, Elizabeth Lavenza, joins the family, following the death of her mother and the remarriage of her father. They become close friends and Frankenstein's mother considers Elizabeth as his 'future wife' (p. 20). They are very different characters, and, in comparing himself to her, Frankenstein introduces contrasts between scientific and artistic endeavour, masculinity and femininity, which Shelley will develop and interrogate later in the novel: 'The world was to me a secret, which I desired to discover; to her it was a vacancy, which she sought to people with imaginations of her own' (p. 21). Frankenstein's aggressively antisocial curiosity, his desire to (as his teacher Waldman later puts it) 'penetrate into the recesses of nature' (p. 30), results in the monstrous events that destroy him and his family. Elizabeth, on the other hand, is at worst a harmless dreamer, rather like Frankenstein's childhood friend Henry Clerval, who is fascinated by tales of chivalry and adventure (p. 21).

Frankenstein seems to have had a model Enlightenment education, one of encouragement and pleasure rather than discipline and rote learning. His enthusiasm for 'natural philosophy' arises mainly by chance: aged 13, he comes across a book by Cornelius Agrippa, a sixteenth-century alchemist and magician (p. 22). As Marilyn Butler points out, a possible influence on *Frankenstein* is Robert Southey's poem 'Cornelius Agrippa' (1799), which describes Agrippa's apprentice reading the magician's book and summoning the devil, who kills him: 'Henceforth let all

young men take heed/ How in a Conjuror's books they read'
(pp. xxvii–xxviii). This poem retells the story of the 'sorcerer's
apprentice', whose curiosity proves fatal; it can also be linked to
the myth of Faust, the Renaissance magician who makes a pact
with the devil. Like both these figures, and like PBS, as an adolescent Frankenstein seeks to use magic to summon 'ghosts or
devils' (p. 24): as an adult he achieves something similar with the
creation of the Creature, a supernaturally powerful being, who is
neither alive nor dead in human terms, and who compares
himself to Satan at several points in the novel. Reading Agrippa
gives Frankenstein a feeling of 'enthusiasm' (p. 22); as discussed
in the previous chapter, this can be a positive term suggesting
passionate inspiration, but it can also have the negative connotations of a dangerous and uncontrolled emotional excitement.
We see later in the novel that Frankenstein's 'enthusiasm' for
uncovering secrets is his undoing.

It is noteworthy that Frankenstein raises the possibility that his
father may be at least partly responsible for not curtailing his
enthusiasm for alchemical texts. Although his father dismisses
Agrippa, he does not explain to him that this occult science is out-
moded; thus Frankenstein continues to study Agrippa's 'wild
fancies', as well as those of Paracelsus and Albertus Magnus,
both alchemists and natural philosophers. He suggests that
without these texts, 'it is even possible, that the train of my ideas
would never have received the fatal impulse that led to my ruin'
(p. 23). This foreshadows the end of the novel, when he refuses to
blame himself for his actions in creating the Creature. He implies
that his father was at fault, and the word 'fatal' may be meant to
suggest not only that the 'impulse' was ruinous or deadly, but that
it was *inevitable*. The adjective 'fatal' comes from the noun 'fate',
which itself comes from the Latin word *fatum*, meaning a sentence or doom of the gods (*OED*). So Frankenstein claims that
his reading directed his ideas in a particular direction, and that he
did not have control over his subsequent actions. Another apparently 'fatal impulse' occurs when, at the age of 15, Frankenstein
witnesses a bolt of lightning strike and destroy an old oak tree
(p. 24), and is thereby introduced (by his father) to some knowledge of electricity and its destructive power.

As an adolescent Frankenstein shares the dreams of the medieval alchemists: discovering the philosopher's stone (believed to turn lead into gold), and the elixir of life (believed to grant immortality): 'the latter obtained my most undivided attention: wealth was an inferior object; but what glory would attend the discovery, if I could banish disease from the human frame, and render man invulnerable to any but a violent death!' (p. 23). As is the case with regard to Walton's desire to reach the North Pole, Frankenstein emphasizes 'glory' as the outcome of his explorations, as well as the benefits to humanity in themselves. This desire for the admiration of others is also apparent later in the novel, when he realizes that he has discovered the secret of life: 'a new species would bless me as its creator and source; many happy and excellent natures would owe their being to me. No father could claim the gratitude of his child so completely as I should deserve theirs' (p. 36). We might see this as rather egotistical: Frankenstein imagines himself being blessed like a deity by his progeny, who would owe him an enormous *debt* of gratitude. Thus Shelley suggests that Frankenstein's goals are at least in part selfish ones. Furthermore, it seems to me that the novel goes further than that by questioning whether those goals are in themselves worthwhile. Mary Shelley's father, the political philosopher William Godwin, had argued in his *Enquiry Concerning Political Justice* (1793), that, through the power of human reason, eventually 'the term of human life may be prolonged, and [. . .] by the immediate operation of the intellect, beyond any limits which we are able to assign' (Shelley 1999, p. 249).[3] Her father's optimistic belief in the positive power of Enlightenment and the inevitability of human improvement is, at the very least, interrogated by Shelley's association of the physically superior Creature (p. 96) with loneliness, violence and misery.

CREATING THE CREATURE

At the age of 17, Frankenstein leaves Geneva to attend university at Ingolstadt in Bavaria. His mother dies of scarlet fever shortly before his departure; it is, of course, fitting that thereafter there should be no maternal presence in the novel. One of *Frankenstein*'s core themes is the importance of domestic affections and what happens when they are absent or ignored. This novel tends to idealize family life, although there are occasional hints about the limitations and problems of this ideal.[4] Frankenstein's move away from a 'secluded and domestic' existence, in which he is 'surrounded by amiable' companions (p. 28), leads to his undoing. At Ingolstadt, he cuts himself off from his family, in order to create a being that, like him, is motherless. And the lack of a nurturing parent is partly what leads to the Creature's destructiveness.

In conflict with this desire for familial closeness and cohesion is Frankenstein's passionate intellectual curiosity: '[I] ardently desired the acquisition of knowledge' (p. 28). As we saw in Chapter 1, 'ardent' is a significant word that applies to Walton as well as to Frankenstein. Like 'enthusiastic', 'ardent' can be positive, meaning 'glowing with passion, animated by keen desire, intensely eager' (*OED*), but it can also have negative connotations of excessive and obsessive desire: wanting something *too much*. During chapters three and four of the novel, as Shelley describes Frankenstein's studies and his creation of the Creature, 'ardent' is used several times and its resonance moves from positive to negative. Initially, it enables his academic progress: his 'application' to work becomes 'so ardent and eager, that the stars often disappeared in the light of morning whilst I was yet engaged in my laboratory'. His 'ardour was indeed the astonishment' of his fellow students (p. 32). However, once he realizes he has discovered the secret of life, his studies become obsessive and damage his health: 'I pursued my undertaking with unremitting ardour. My cheek had grown pale with study, and my person had become emaciated with confinement' (p. 36). Frankenstein starts to resemble the corpses that he is experimenting on, suggesting his increasing alienation from the everyday world. And when the Creature has been created, he realizes that he has gone too far: 'I had deprived myself of rest and health. I had desired it [creating life] with an ardour that far exceeded moderation; but now that I had finished, the beauty of the dream vanished, and breathless horror and disgust filled my heart' (p. 39). His 'ardour', his passionate and excessive desire for knowledge and glory, takes him into a dream world and leads him to neglect himself and his family. Once the Creature has been created, Frankenstein re-enters a world of 'normal' human responses, where the sight of such a being provokes 'horror and disgust'. 'Breathless' suggests fear and anticipation, but also a state akin to death; by giving life ('breath') to the Creature, he has started a deadly sequence of events.

So where does this ardency, this dream-like state, come from? We have already seen that as an adolescent Frankenstein dreamed of gaining glory by discovering the secret of eternal life, and that in maturity he imagines the enormous gratitude of his manufactured children. We might see this ardency, therefore, as the result of a deep-seated desire to have his ego acknowledged and celebrated by others. But there is more to it than that: it is also to do with power and sexuality. When Frankenstein arrives at university, his view that the alchemical dreams of his youth were chimerical is confirmed by one of the professors; and at first he has no enthusiasm for 'modern natural philosophy' because he sees it as unambitious in comparison. However, under the tutelage and friendship of the chemist Waldman, he realizes this view to be mistaken. Waldman tells him that

> these philosophers, whose hands seem only made to dabble in dirt, and their eyes to pore over the microscope or crucible, have indeed performed miracles. They penetrate into the recesses of nature, and shew how she works in her hiding places. They ascend into the heavens; they have discovered how the blood circulates, and the nature of the air we breathe. They have acquired new and almost unlimited powers; they can command the thunders of heaven, mimic the earthquake, and even mock the invisible world with its own shadows. (pp. 30–31)

This is a very important passage. As several critics have noted, it is influenced by the eminent chemist Humphry Davy's *A Lecture, Introductory to a Course of Lectures on Chemistry* (1802) (Shelley 1999, p. 22; Mellor 1989, pp. 91–95). Waldman refers to various modern scientific discoveries and inventions, including the hot-air balloon, explosives and illusionist exhibitions such as magic-lantern shows (for a full list of allusions, see Shelley 1996a, p. 33).

Two aspects of the passage's language are noteworthy: it uses *religious* terms to emphasize human power; and it is *gendered*. The language echoes that of Davy, who had emphasized the 'creative' power of the modern chemist to change the world, and repre-sented him as mastering a feminized nature (Mellor 1989, p. 93). Although it can be used in a secular context, the primary meaning of 'miracle' (from the Latin *miraculum*, meaning 'object of wonder') is 'a marvellous event not ascribable to human power or the operation of any natural force and therefore attributed to supernatural, esp. divine, agency' (*OED*). Scientists, Waldman claims, have attained powers hitherto associated with the divine. The Bible describes Jesus performing miracles that prove him to be the son of God and 'ascended into heaven' suggests His Ascension following His crucifixion. This suggests that, like Jesus, modern natural philosophers are both men and gods. Furthermore, the ability to 'command the thunders' alludes to Zeus/Jupiter, the king of the gods in classical mythology, whose weapon was the thun-derbolt. Such is the power of these philosophers that 'the invisible world', associated with the spiritual and the unknown, is now 'mocked' – controlled and replicated – by human ingenuity.

Waldman not only emphasizes the divinity of human power, its ability to transgress earthly limitations, but also its masculin-ity. The mysterious workings of female nature are exposed by male experimentation, and her 'recesses' are 'penetrated', an obvious sexual allusion. Frankenstein himself uses similar lan-guage when describing the scientific explorations that led to his creation of the Creature: 'The moon gazed on my midnight labours, while, with unrelaxed and breathless eagerness, I pursued nature to her hiding places' (p. 36). Frankenstein is excited, perhaps sexually excited ('unrelaxed' (turgid/erect) and 'breathless'), by his night time pursuit of a female nature in order to uncover her secrets; that nature seeks to hide from her pursuer raises the prospect of a violent rape. Fascinatingly, this sexual language soon becomes caught up in macabre descriptions of death and putrefaction:

Who shall conceive the horrors of my secret toil, as I dabbled among the unhallowed damps of the grave, or tortured the living animal to animate the lifeless clay? [. . .] [A] resistless, and almost frantic impulse, urged me forward; I seemed to have lost all soul or sensation but for this one pursuit. It was indeed but a passing trance, that only made me feel with renewed acuteness so soon as, the unnatural stimulus ceasing to operate, I had returned to my old habits. I collected bones from charnel houses; and disturbed, with profane fingers, the tremendous secrets of the human frame. In a solitary chamber, or rather cell [. . .] I kept my workshop of filthy creation; my eyeballs were starting from their sockets in attending to the details of my employment. The dissecting room and the slaughter-house furnished many of my materials; and often did my human nature turn with loathing from my occupation, whilst, still urged on by an eagerness which perpetually increased, I brought my work near to a conclusion. (p. 36)

Whereas Waldman's panegyric on modern science quickly moved away from the image of 'philosophers [. . .] dabbl[ing] in dirt' to imagine their supernatural powers, this passage lingers on the earthly and the deathly. The language of religious transcendence has been replaced by that of religious desecration: Frankenstein haunts 'unhallowed' (unholy) places, and his 'profane' (unholy) fingers disturb the 'tremendous [literally meaning 'to be trembled at'] secrets of the human frame'; again, there is a rather unsettling hint of violent penetration about this image. Frankenstein's obsession at this point in the narrative is all-consuming, rather like Walton's, and it prevents him from thinking rationally. It is 'resistless', a 'trance', an 'unnatural stimulus' that works against 'human nature' and engulfs his 'soul', suggesting that he is engaged in something blasphemous and devilish. The pressing nature of this 'stimulus' ('urged me forward') also implies sexual excitement, and the image of an aroused and stimulated Frankenstein working in his 'solitary chamber' suggests masturbation, sexual activity that does not require anyone else but is here procreative rather than sterile. Without necessarily doubting the accuracy of Frankenstein's account, we should be aware that in this passage he may be seeking to suggest that he was not responsible for his actions, the victim of a fatal ('resistless') obsession, and therefore should not be blamed for the Creature's crimes.

Frankenstein also appears in this passage as someone whose activities have corrupted him, making him *monstrous*. His work is secret and solitary – we go on to find out that he has been utterly neglecting his family – and involves tormenting animals, presumably through live dissections. As we discover later in the novel, the creation of life can be highly destructive. Just before the passage, Frankenstein describes himself as corpse-like ('pale' and 'emaciated'), and the striking image of his own eyeballs 'starting out of their sockets' when faced with the horror of his surroundings and activities, emphasizes his connection to the dismembered corpses that he experiments on. Furthermore, it also links him to the Creature itself, whose yellow, watery eyes, set in 'dun white sockets' are so disturbing (pp. 38–39). This suggests that the fact that he was in a 'trance' is significant, for the word is related to the Old French *transe*, meaning the passage from life to death, and the Latin *transire*, meaning to pass over or to cross. 'Penetrating' Nature's 'recesses' is shown to involve transgressing the boundaries of life and death, an activity that is not only 'filthy' and distasteful, but also dangerous, corrupting and threatening to his humanity.

This imagery of corruption, death and sexuality reaches a disturbing climax in the dream that Frankenstein experiences shortly after giving life to the Creature:

> I saw Elizabeth, in the bloom of health, walking in the streets of Ingolstadt. Delighted and surprised, I embraced her; but as I imprinted the first kiss on her lips, they became livid with the hue of death; her features appeared to change, and I thought that I held the corpse of my dead mother in my arms; a shroud enveloped her form, and I saw the grave-worms crawling in the folds of the flannel. (p. 39)

This passage highlights two important aspects of Frankenstein's character and the novel's themes. The first is, as Anne K. Mellor suggests, 'the destruction of the female implicit in Frankenstein's usurpation of the natural mode of human reproduction' (1989, p. 115). Frankenstein's aggressively masculine science not only seeks violently to dominate a maternal nature, but also to make women unnecessary to society by replicating their ability to reproduce. This is symbolized by his deathly kiss, transforming his future wife into his mother's corpse, and prefigures the terrible effect that the creation of the Creature has on his whole family. The second aspect is the association of sexual desire, particularly transgressive desire, with imagery of putrefaction and death (consider in particular the vaginal 'folds of the flannel' and the phallic 'grave-worms'). It reflects, perhaps, the way in which Frankenstein's sexual desire for his cousin, and possibly for his mother, is repressed and sublimated into his scientific activities. The disturbingly close-knit nature of Frankenstein's family (where it is assumed that he will marry the cousin who has been brought up as his sister), and the consequent anxieties about incest, may therefore be seen as the repressed *stimulus* for his endeavours, rather than their opposite. His ardent pursuit of nature to 'her hiding places', his poking and prodding of corpses, is at root libidinous (sexual): it manifests what Sigmund Freud termed 'Eros', the drive to create and preserve life. However, for Frankenstein, the erotic is profoundly linked to Freud's 'death drive', 'Thanatos', which is aggressive and destructive, and seeks to break down the units of life formed by Eros. In order to create life, Frankenstein has had to wallow in death and dismemberment; dissecting living animals and pulling corpses apart in order to put together the Creature. There is a hint slightly earlier in the text that these researches may reflect a desire to resurrect his mother: 'I thought, that if I could bestow animation upon lifeless matter, I might in process of time [. . .] renew life where death had apparently devoted the body to corruption' (p. 36). Frankenstein's dream, which follows his horror and disgust at the now living body of the Creature, expresses his feeling that rather than creating or renewing life, he has created a grotesque parody of it. It also suggests, though, that (parody or not) the existence of the Creature is the product of Frankenstein's own inability properly to distinguish between the erotic and the destructive, a blurring of boundaries on which the novel bases itself.

FRANKENSTEIN'S FAMILY

In comparison to the three main characters of the novel – male, separate from normal society and morally ambivalent – the various family members who appear are very much underdrawn, and to a large extent idealized. Frankenstein's narrative is, of course, retrospective, and it is possible that his very positive description of his family is coloured by his sense of guilt and loss. Psychologically speaking, they are static; they do not change or develop as characters during the course of the narrative, but simply display their essential qualities. Frankenstein's father is an exemplary public servant (p. 18), who saves the daughter of his dead friend Beaufort from life as 'an orphan and a beggar' (p. 19) and ends up marrying her. He also takes in Elizabeth Lavenza, the daughter of his dead sister, whom Frankenstein eventually marries. Elizabeth is described as immensely attractive in body and mind: lively, passionate, affectionate, graceful, imaginative, and hard-working (pp. 20–21). We do not see much of Frankenstein's mother because she dies so early in the narrative, but we know that she is brave and benevolent. His brother Ernest is sickly but of a 'gentle' disposition and his youngest brother is 'beautiful' and 'endearing' (p. 25). Clerval, the poet and linguist, who is virtually a family member, has 'singular talent and fancy' (p. 21); his goodness, loyalty and particularly his capacity for imaginative sympathy enables Frankenstein to recover from his physical illness and mental anguish after creating the Creature, and once more to enjoy nature and literature (pp. 43–51). Justine, who joins the family as a servant after Frankenstein has left Geneva, is 'very clever and gentle, and extremely pretty' (p. 47), and behaves with exemplary dignity and fortitude throughout her trial.

It can be strangely easy to forget that this novel is not simply about the battle between two tormented and powerful beings, but the story of how an ostensibly perfect family is utterly destroyed by the ambition of one of its members. The fact that this familial idyll is highly transient is registered by an allusion early on in Frankenstein's narrative, when he mentions his regrets about leaving to study at Ingolstadt: 'I loved my brothers, Elizabeth, and Clerval; these were "old familiar faces" ' (p. 28). This refers to the title and refrain of a popular poem by Charles Lamb (1775–1834), first published in 1798 (Lloyd and Lamb 1798, pp. 89–91). Lamb's poem is a disturbingly frank and honest account of his own unhappiness and sense of loss.[5] Its resonance with *Frankenstein* is remarkable. Here is the opening stanza:

Where are they gone; the old familiar faces?
I had a mother, but she died, and left me,
Died prematurely in a day of horrors–
All, all are gone, the old familiar faces. (ll. 1–4)

Lamb links his mother's death to 'horror' because she was murdered in 1796 by her daughter and his sister, Mary, who was suffering from a fit of insanity. In 1800, Lamb became a friend of William Godwin, who in 1807 published *Tales from Shakespeare*, written partly by Lamb but mainly by his sister (Mellor 1989, pp. 5–6; Burton 2004, pp. 157–58, 239–40). Shelley would have met Lamb numerous times as she was growing up and it seems highly likely that she would have known about the familial trauma that lay behind the poem. Frankenstein's 'day of horrors' is the day he creates the Creature, but, as we have seen, his dream links this to the death of his mother, who has also died 'prematurely'. The poem's speaker goes on to lament the loss of his 'playmates' and 'companions' (l. 5) from his happy childhood, and describes how he cannot see the woman he loves (ll. 11–12), prefiguring Frankenstein's separation from Elizabeth and Clerval and their eventual deaths.

The speaker also has 'a friend', whom he leaves 'abruptly / [. . .] to muse on the old familiar faces' (ll. 15–16); he wishes this friend could have been born in his 'father's dwelling', 'so might we talk of the old familiar faces' (ll. 21–22). Perhaps this does not fit quite so neatly with *Frankenstein* as do the earlier stanzas, but it still has some interesting resonance. We can imagine the friend as Clerval, neglected by Frankenstein as he pursues his obsession, and who is virtually a family member. But what about the Creature? Frankenstein certainly 'abruptly' decides to have nothing to do with him, failing in his duty to nurture his creation.

As we shall see, Frankenstein and the Creature are very strongly linked in all kinds of ways; the Creature is in a sense 'more than a brother', as he is Frankenstein's offspring. A being born in his 'father's dwelling' would presumably be the son that his family would have wished him to have, the fruit of the union between him and Elizabeth. Thus this allusion may look forward to the situation that Frankenstein finds himself in much later in the novel, and comment on the way in which the creation of the Creature disrupts 'normal' family ties.

Towards the end of the poem, the speaker, stricken by loss and absence, seeks to return to familial connections that have been irretrievably broken:

> Ghost-like, I pac'd round the haunts of my childhood.
> Earth seem'd a desert I was bound to traverse,
> Seeking to find the old familiar faces. (ll. 17–19)

Like a ghost, the speaker is caught between death and life, alienated from all other beings and will never find rest, at least not while on 'Earth': this is not only appropriate to Frankenstein, but also to the Creature. In particular, it prefigures Frankenstein's situation and language after the deaths of his family: 'Now my wanderings began [. . .] I have traversed a vast portion of the earth, and have endured all the hardships which travellers, in deserts and barbarous countries, are wont to meet' (p. 171). Here he is talking about the searching for the Creature, but the disturbing thing is that the Creature, although 'Other' and alien, is also a familiar and *familial* face, albeit one that for much of the novel Frankenstein wants to repress. The speaker of Lamb's poem laments that all 'familiar faces' have 'departed' and that '*some are taken from me*' (l. 24; italics in original). By taking Frankenstein's family from him, the Creature effectively replaces them, ensuring that his creator is *bonded* to him, even if those are bonds of hate rather than of love. In pursuing the Creature, Frankenstein is also pursuing the family he has lost.

After Frankenstein's mother, the next 'familiar face' to be lost is William, whom we later find out to have been throttled by the Creature. In the face of this tragedy, Frankenstein's family maintain their essential goodness; his father exhorts him to come home, 'not brooding thoughts of vengeance against the assassin, but with feelings of peace and gentleness, that will heal, instead of festering the wounds of our minds' (p. 53). Understandably, before long Frankenstein will indeed be 'brooding' on the prospect of avenging himself against the Creature. Although his father seems willing to allow Justine to be convicted of William's murder, on highly circumstantial evidence, Elizabeth shows her benevolence by refusing to believe her guilt, even before knowing Frankenstein's views. The novel makes much of Justine's innocence and goodness, to the extent that it is hard to imagine the judges and 'the popular voice' being willing to condemn her even before she confesses (p. 64). As with the other members of Frankenstein's family, and with the Creature's 'family', the De Laceys, her moral qualities are exemplified by her appearance, and she offers a sharp contrast to the moral and physical monstrousness of the real murderer: her expression is 'uncommonly lovely'; her 'open and capacious forehead' reveals her intelligence; 'her hair [i]s rich dark auburn, her complexion fair, and her figure slight and graceful' (p. 60). In one sense, the court judges her by appearances, basing its condemnation on the locket that the Creature has planted on her and her confused manner: the confession simply tells it what it already thinks it knows. In another sense, though, the court signally *fails* to judge on appearances, refusing to read Justine's beauty as an index of her morality. *Frankenstein* is deeply concerned with issues of misjudgement and misinterpretation: during his early life, the Creature is frequently blamed and punished for his appearance, rather than his actions, but when he becomes morally monstrous, he gets away without punishment, at least for a while.

What I find particularly interesting about the passages surrounding Justine's trial and execution is that, although most of the dialogue is between Elizabeth and Justine, who behave with predictably exemplary goodness and fortitude, the narrative's focus is very much on Frankenstein. This is not simply because events are being told from his perspective, but also because of the novel's concerns. During the trial, he suffers 'living torture', knowing that William's death and possibly Justine's may be the result of his 'curiosity and lawless devices' (p. 61) ('devices', here, means projects or inventions). This is highly understandable, but what seems excessive is his emphatic insistence that his sufferings are more severe than Justine's:

> I could not sustain the horror of my situation; and when I per-ceived that the popular voice, and the countenance of the judges, had already condemned my unhappy victim, I rushed out of the court in agony. The tortures of the accused did not equal mine; she was sustained by innocence, but the fangs of remorse tore my bosom, and would not forego their hold. (p. 64)

Note the emphasis here on '*my* situation', *my* 'agony', and *my* 'tortures'. When Elizabeth and Justine discuss despair and resig-nation, Frankenstein becomes strangely angry because he feels the words do not reflect the depth of his suffering:

> Despair! Who dared to talk of that? The poor victim, who on the morrow was to pass the dreary boundary between life and death, felt not as I did, such deep and bitter agony. (p. 67)

This emphasis on his own sufferings might seem to make sense in religious terms; Justine will die without having sinned, and of course it is only the fact that a priest threatens her with 'excom-munication and hell fire' that makes her confess (p. 66). At least she will cross the 'boundary between life and death' with a clear conscience, in comparison to Frankenstein's guilt for meddling with that boundary. Perhaps he fears that he will die without absolution and go to hell. And yet the 1818 text of *Frankenstein* is notably unreligious: it contains relatively little emphasis on Frankenstein as sinning against God and he seems to have little fear of what will happen to him in the afterlife. So there must be something else going on here. One way of making sense of this would simply be to see this hyperbole as an expression of Frankenstein's egotistical character: self-involved, self-obsessed, and self-pitying. A more productive approach, though, might be to think about what this novel is actually interested in exploring.

This novel does not *care* very much about the sufferings of Frankenstein's family because those sufferings do not directly bear upon its Gothic focus on transgression and the resulting moral issues. Justine is unambiguously a victim, without any responsibility for her fate, and therefore her experience, however horrible, is not interesting. Frankenstein and the Creature, on the other hand, are not easily categorizable: they are suffering 'victims', but they are also 'villains' who cause intense sufferings to others and whose actions ask possibly irresolvable questions about responsibility. Is the Creature guilty, given that he commits the physical acts of murder? Or is he merely the victim of circumstances? Is Frankenstein ultimately the villain of the piece, given that he lets the Creature loose into the world? Or, again, is he impelled by circumstances to embark on this disastrous endeavour? One of the things that makes *Frankenstein* a great novel is its *ambivalence*: its refusal to give definitive answers to these and other questions.

This relative lack of interest in the experiences of Frankenstein's family is apparent in the ways in which the other deaths are described, and is not simply a result of the first-person narrative. Clerval's death takes place 'off camera', as it were; we see the body briefly and know that he has been throttled. The focus, again, is on Frankenstein's guilt, although his friend later reappears as an imagined ghost figure symbolizing this (pp. 153–54). Similarly, although we get more direct insight into Elizabeth through the two letters that she sends to Frankenstein, they simply serve to emphasize her goodness and altruism, and, as with Clerval, when she dies Frankenstein and the reader sees the corpse, not the murder (p. 165). His father's death is quickly described in a short paragraph (pp. 167–68), and we never find out what eventually happens to Ernest; the last we hear of him is that he 'yet lived' after his father's death. Perhaps there is more to say about these characters. In fact, an interesting way of reading the novel 'against the grain' would be to try to focus much more on, or even to reconstruct, the perspectives and experiences of Frankenstein's family. But, for the purposes of this study, our focus has to be on Frankenstein's experience. This novel is not interested in the sufferings of innocents, except in as far as they affect its ambiguous, tormented protagonists and illuminate its dark themes.

FRANKENSTEIN'S DOUBLES

It is a truism of cultural history that writers of the Romantic period were fascinated by the figure of the solitary (male) genius who stands apart from normal society. This fascination led to a wide array of responses, ranging from the consecration of the creative artist as an inspired being in aesthetic theory (see, for example, PBS's 'A Defence of Poetry' (1821)) to the transgressive, 'Satanic' protagonists of Byron's poetry (for example, *The Corsair* (1814), *Manfred* (1817), and *Cain* (1821)). One of the principal questions asked by *Frankenstein* is whether its protagonist is a heroic genius, a 'divine wanderer' or a foolish and selfish antihero/villain. *Frankenstein* can be read as a critique of Romantic-period representations of the divine creativity of genius, presenting a solitary and egotistical man pursuing his obsessive explorations to the neglect of all other matters, and achieving his goals only at the cost of a great deal of death and destruction. However, there is also meant to be something fascinating and deeply impressive about Frankenstein; he is a highly ambivalent figure. Shelley reflects and develops this ambivalence by offering several other characters as points of comparison – the Creature, Clerval, and (as I discussed in the previous chapter) Walton – and also by alluding to several other 'genius' figures from outside the novel.

As various critics have discussed, there is plenty of evidence that the character and background of Frankenstein shares similarities with that of PBS. He used 'Victor' as a pseudonym during his youth and his first publication was *Original Poetry; by Victor and Cazire* (1810). His favourite among his four sisters was called Elizabeth. Nora Crook notes that he told Godwin in 1812 that 'Paracelsus and Albertus Magnus had been among his favourite boyhood reading' (Shelley 1996a, p. 26). Frankenstein's youthful fantasies of 'the raising of ghosts or devils' (p. 24) echo passages from PBS's poems *Alastor* (1816) and 'Hymn to Intellectual Beauty' (1817):

I have made my bed
In charnels and on coffins, where black death

46

Keeps record of the trophies won from thee [Mother Nature],
Hoping to still these obstinate questionings
Of thee and thine, by forcing some lone ghost,
Thy messenger, to render up the tale
Of what we are. (Shelley 2002, p. 74, ll. 22–29)

The speaker here is the narrator of *Alastor*, who is about to tell
the story of a solitary poet, a 'lovely youth', who avoids real
human sympathy in favour of a being created by his imagination;
unable to find such a being, 'he descends to an untimely grave'
(Shelley 2002, p. 73). The parallels between this story and
Frankenstein are interesting, although the relationship between
the narrator of Alastor and the protagonist-poet is unclear and
debated by critics. In the passage quoted, PBS seems to be speaking autobiographically. There is a hint of the connection between
sex and death made in Frankenstein ('made my bed'), and this is
also apparent in the dream experienced by the poet protagonist
of *Alastor*, when he imagines embracing a 'veiled maid [. . .]
herself a poet' before sinking into darkness and 'vacancy' (ll.
161–91). There is also an emphasis on curiosity: seeking to *force*
the dead to give up the secrets of nature, life and human identity
('what we are'), which is exactly what Frankenstein does.[6]

PBS was also keenly interested in modern natural philosophy,
particularly chemistry, performing numerous experiments during
his time at Oxford, and, as recounted by his friend Thomas
Jefferson Hogg in 1832, talked with tremendous enthusiasm
about the ways in which various scientific discoveries and
inventions (including electricity) could greatly improve human
existence (Mullan 1996, vol. 1, pp. 56–63). Above all, PBS was
represented by his contemporaries and at times by himself as an
enthusiast, a visionary who approached life, politics and literature
with a dreamy eagerness and idealism that occasionally went too
far. The radical essayist William Hazlitt, for example, who was
relatively sympathetic to PBS's politics, wrote in 1821 that PBS
'has a fire in his eye, a fever in his blood, a maggot in his brain, a
hectic flutter in his speech, which mark out the philosophic
fanatic', suggesting that (rather like Walton and Frankenstein)
there was something disturbingly excessive and feverish about the

poet's enthusiasms. In the same essay, Hazlitt develops this point with reference to a series of metaphors from the natural sciences, presenting PBS as a scientific charlatan conducting 'electrical experiments in morals and philosophy', which 'though they may scorch other people [. . .] are to him harmless amusements' (Hazlitt 1930–33, vol. 7, pp. 148–49). It is hard not to see the figure of Victor Frankenstein lurking behind this imagery.[7] Anne K. Mellor argues that 'Mary [. . .] had come to suspect that in Percy's case, [his abstract ideals] sometimes masked an emotional narcissism, an unwillingness to confront the origins of his own desires or the impact of his demands on those most dependent upon him' (1989, p. 73). This is borne out by evidence of his treatment of both his wives. I am not suggesting that Shelley meant Victor Frankenstein to be a direct representation of PBS, but his characterization as an obsessional, transgressive visionary is undoubtedly informed by her experience of her husband.

The full title of Shelley's novel is *Frankenstein; or, the Modern Prometheus*. In Greek mythology, Prometheus was a Titan, one of the giants who originally controlled the universe and who were overthrown by Zeus, the king of the gods. He stole fire from Mount Olympus, the home of the gods, to give to a suffering and neglected humanity, shivering in the cold. Zeus punished him by chaining him to Mount Caucasus, where every day an eagle would peck at his liver, which would regrow to be pecked again the following day. One version of this story is told by the Ancient Greek dramatist Aeschylus in *Prometheus Bound*, which both Byron and PBS responded to in poetry. The protagonist of Byron's 'Prometheus' (1816), through his pity, suffering and inability to escape from his fate, becomes an emblem of the human condition. In PBS's *Prometheus Unbound* (1820), Prometheus forgives his oppressor, Zeus, and this allows both his freedom and that of the human race from the injustices of power. Prometheus is represented as a heroic figure, a bearer of Enlightenment, liberty and progress. This might well be a partial reflection of Frankenstein's character, or at least how he sees himself before he actually creates the Creature.

However, in the version of the legend by the Roman poet Ovid, Prometheus is represented as a figure who may have created human life by animating clay with 'particles of heavenly fire', suggesting a link with Frankenstein's use of electricity (Pollin, pp. 102–03). Thus Mary Shelley seems to have had both myths in mind when writing the novel, and her treatment of Prometheus is much more ambivalent than that of Byron and PBS. Both poets reflected on how the only suffering caused by the original Prometheus was to himself, whereas in Shelley's novel, Frankenstein's actions cause a great deal of suffering to others as well, whatever his intentions. The word 'modern' in the subtitle suggests not only that she is bringing the myth into a contemporary setting, but perhaps also that Frankenstein is a different sort of Promethean figure, one at least partially lacking in the altruistic heroic virtue of the original. 'Modern' may designate a decline into selfishness and Frankenstein may be more a parody of Prometheus than an updated version.

Other important literary influences on *Frankenstein* include the novels of Shelley's father William Godwin, particularly *Caleb Williams* (1794) and *St Leon* (1799), and 'Pygmalion et Galatée' (1802) by Madame de Genlis (Pollin, pp. 100–01), but the most significant is undoubtedly John Milton's epic poem *Paradise Lost* (1667). Milton sought to 'justify the ways of God to men' (I, l. 26) – to explain why God allows evil to exist – by retelling the story of Satan's rebellion and the expulsion of Adam and Eve from the Garden of Eden. This was not simply a theological project, but a *political* one. Milton was a republican who was trying to make sense of the failure of the English Revolution and the Restoration of the monarchy in 1660. One of the three books that the Creature discovers in the De Laceys' cottage, *Paradise Lost* is alluded to numerous times throughout the novel, and provides the epigraph to the 1818 edition:

Did I request thee, Maker, from my clay
To mould Me man? Did I solicit thee
From darkness to promote me? (p. 1)

This places Frankenstein as God, and the Creature as Adam, and is echoed by the Creature at several points in the novel. Frankenstein may have the divine power to create life, but, as the

Creature points out, he is a poor excuse for a God, making no efforts to nurture or protect his creation, and leaving it solitary in a hostile world. Adam had to commit the sin of disobedience before being cast out of Eden, whereas the Creature is immediately disowned by his creator. And whereas Adam had Eve as a companion, Frankenstein refuses to make the Creature a wife.

A more appropriate parallel for Frankenstein from *Paradise Lost* may be the figure of Satan, to whom the Creature also compares *himself* at several points in his narrative. Milton's Satan is a glorious angel who seeks to challenge God's power and is therefore cast out of heaven; his Fall comes from his arrogant refusal to accept the limits of his power. Satan was a figure of great interest to several of the Romantics, particularly because of his revolt against his established authority. William Blake stated in *The Marriage of Heaven and Hell* (1790) that Milton 'wrote in fetters when he wrote of angels and God, and at liberty when of devils and Hell [. . .] because he was a true poet, and of the Devil's party without knowing it' (Blake 2007, p. 113). Godwin argued in *Political Justice* (1793) that Satan's rebellion against God showed him to have an innate sense of justice: 'he bore his torments with fortitude, because he disdained to be subdued by despotic power' (Shelley 1999, p. 250). In the preface to *Prometheus Unbound*, PBS describes Satan as 'the hero' of *Paradise Lost*, although he suggests that Prometheus is a 'more poetical character': they are both courageous and opposed to 'omnipotent force', but Prometheus lacks Satan's dark qualities (Shelley 2002, pp. 206–07). Attitudes to Satan became, to a certain extent, an index of a poet's politics. Hence the conservative poet Robert Southey (1774–1843), horrified by the transgressive strain in the poetry of Byron and Shelley, attacked what he called the 'Satanic school' of poetry: 'men of diseased hearts and depraved imaginations [who] [. . .] have rebelled against the holiest ordinances of human society' (Southey 1838, vol. 10, pp. 205–06).

We might see Frankenstein as sharing the ambivalence of Milton's Satan: both characters exhibit a complex mixture of positive and negative qualities, both aspire to power and glory, both transgress boundaries that are inscribed by God, and both find that their aspirations lead to great suffering. Shortly before his death, Frankenstein makes the connection explicitly to Walton: 'like the archangel who aspired to omnipotence, I am chained in an eternal hell. [. . .] I trod heaven in my thoughts [. . .] but how am I sunk!' (p. 180). His increasing suffering and isolation following the creation of the Creature link to Satan's banishment from heaven after his transgression. Following the execution of Justine, for example, Frankenstein is wracked with guilt:

> Sleep fled from my eyes; I wandered like an evil spirit, for I had committed deeds of mischief beyond description horrible, and more, much more, (I persuaded myself) was yet behind [i.e. to come]. Yet my heart overflowed with kindness, and the love of virtue. I had begun life with benevolent intentions, and thirsted for the moment when I should put them in practice [. . .] I was seized by remorse and the sense of guilt, which hurried me away to a hell of intense tortures, such as no language can describe. (p. 69)

In contrast to the self-justification that sometimes characterizes Frankenstein's narrative, here he describes himself as suffering an intense guilt, so intense that he might be considered to be taking too much responsibility for the deaths of William and Justine. The comparison to an 'evil spirit' and the reference to a personal 'hell' strongly links Frankenstein to his creation, who later says that 'like the arch fiend [Satan], [I] bore a hell within me' (p. 111). This is one of the most interesting aspects of the novel: although Frankenstein represents the Creature as a vile wretch, to be execrated and destroyed, and although the Creature hates the creator who abandoned him and seeks vengeance, there are such strong links and parallels between the two that they become doubles of one another, joined by bonds of hatred and alienation and pursuing each other across the world. Frankenstein writes here as if *he* had committed the Creature's murders, and goes on to call himself 'the author [creator] of unalterable evils' (p. 70). Later in the narrative, after Clerval's death, Frankenstein speaks remorsefully of his 'murderous machinations' (p. 148) and 'infernal [hellish] machinations' (p. 154). Given that a 'machination' normally refers to a malicious plot or stratagem, these phrases make it sound as if Frankenstein actually planned the deaths of his family, again conflating his intentions with those of the Creature. Furthermore, Frankenstein's insistence that his intentions were originally 'benevolent' is also echoed by the Creature later in the story (pp. 78, 119, 189).

These similarities are important. After all, what supposedly makes the Creature 'monstrous' is that he is unnaturally different from, 'Other' to, all living beings (the Latin word *monstrosus* means 'portentous, unnatural, strange' (*OED*)). The link between him and Frankenstein might suggest two things: first, that there is something rather monstrous about Frankenstein, and second that the Creature is considerably more human than his exterior implies. Following the murder of William, Frankenstein experiences a moment of self-awareness:

> I considered the being whom I had cast among mankind, and endowed with the will and power to effect purposes of horror, such as the deed which he had now done, nearly in the light of my own vampire, my own spirit let loose from the grave, and forced to destroy all that was dear to me. (p. 57)

There is an emphasis on personal responsibility here ('I had cast' and '[I had] endowed') and there is also interesting ambiguity. Are the 'purposes of horror' the Creature's, or Frankenstein's? As various critics have pointed out, the Creature can be seen as Frankenstein's dark alter ego ('my own vampire') running amok among his family and acting out his repressed desires (see, for example, Cantor 1984, p. 117). We might at this point recall that in the Book of Genesis, God creates Man 'in his own image'. Thus it is the Creature, rather than Frankenstein, who is 'with' Elizabeth on her wedding night, with her murder replacing, or perhaps symbolically replicating, her deflowering. Frankenstein and his creation often experience similar feelings and use similar language to express them: for example, in their response to the onset of Spring (pp. 51, 92). In particular, they are strongly linked by a shared rhetoric of violence and despair. The scientist's desire to revenge himself on the Creature makes *him* inhuman and monstrous: 'I gnashed my teeth, my eyes became inflamed [. . .] [and] my hatred and revenge burst all bounds of moderation' (p. 71). Similarly, after Frankenstein destroys his bride, the Creature 'gnashed his teeth in the impotence of anger', stating, '[y]ou can blast my other passions; but revenge remains [. . .] you, my tyrant and tormentor, shall curse the sun that gazes on your misery' (p. 140). Each torments and tyrannizes the other, binding them together in a spiralling cycle of violence that can only end in their deaths. In PBS's *Prometheus Unbound*, Prometheus is able to forgive his tyrant and tormentor, Jupiter, by revoking the curse that he made at the start of his suffering. This breaks the cycle and allows the universe to enter a new golden age of freedom and justice. Shelley's novel offers no such hope.

An important word that links Frankenstein and the Creature is 'wretch', which has a fascinating etymology and range of meanings. The *OED* gives three main definitions. The first, obsolete and coming from the Old English, is 'one driven out of or away from his native country; a banished person; an exile'; the second is 'one who is sunk in deep distress'; and the third is 'a vile, sorry, or despicable person'. The word (and its cognates) is used a great deal in *Frankenstein*, perhaps overused, but all three meanings are important to the novel and serve to link its main characters. Frankenstein describes the Creature as a 'wretch' (using the third meaning) on numerous occasions: he does so four times in two pages when describing his feelings after creating him (pp. 39–40). This suggests, I think, both Frankenstein's visceral disgust at the Creature's 'hideous' appearance, but also the fact that the story is being told retrospectively; thus his description of the Creature is coloured by his experience of the Creature's crimes. However, when Frankenstein is first rescued by Walton and his crew, he is described as being in a 'wretched' condition (the second meaning) (p. 13), damaged in body and mind by his pursuit of the Creature. Frankenstein often uses the word to describe himself in the same way: returning to his house after fleeing from the Creature, he sleeps 'wretchedly' (p. 40); wandering over the Alps after the death of William, he 'foresaw obscurely that I was destined to become the most wretched of human beings' (p. 55); following the execution of Justine, he states that 'I was a wretch, and none ever conceived of the misery that I then endured' (p. 68).

Frankenstein's use of 'wretch' expresses, therefore, his 'Othering' of the Creature. (Notably both William and Walton also apply this word to the Creature, suggesting that they share Frankenstein's attitude.) You are a wretch, he says to his creation, in that you are hideous, malignant, and hateful; on the other hand, I am a wretch in that I am suffering and alone. The Creature's narrative makes this binary contrast untenable and emphasizes the slippage between the two meanings. The Creature sees himself as born 'wretched' (suffering) and therefore hated by humanity as a low creature (p. 77). Wandering in the forest shortly after his creation, he is 'a poor, helpless, miserable wretch' (p. 80), and he uses the word several times in the following pages to describe his lonely existence. After Frankenstein has torn his bride to pieces, he turns the word against his creator, threatening to make him 'so wretched that the light of day will be hateful to [him]' (p. 140), just as it was to the Creature shortly after his creation (p. 80). After all, he asks, 'are you to be happy, while I grovel in the intensity of my wretchedness?' (p. 140). The Creature, therefore, inverts Frankenstein's claim. I am a wretch, he says, in that I am suffering and alone and hated by humanity and therefore I will make you, my creator, similarly wretched (suffering) by committing wretched (evil) actions. When Frankenstein swears a dramatic oath of vengeance at the cemetery where his family are buried, the Creature tells him triumphantly that 'I am satisfied: miserable wretch! you have determined to live and I am satisfied' (p. 172). Here 'wretch' describes Frankenstein's desolate condition, but is also a term of execration and hate. The Creature's argument throughout the novel is that one sort of wretchedness (misery) will lead to the other sort (evil), and, unlike Frankenstein, he acknowledges his wretched transgressions: 'it is true that I am a wretch. I have murdered the lovely and helpless' (p. 190).

But what of the obsolete meaning of 'wretch': 'a banished person, an exile'? This is from the Old English, *wrecca* or *wraecca*, meaning 'exile, adventurer, knight errant' (the latter is 'a knight of mediæval romance who wandered in search of adventures and opportunities for deeds of bravery and chivalry'; in modern

German *recke* means warrior or hero). This meaning could apply to all three main characters. Frankenstein and Walton are self-exiles, who travel away from their homes in search of knowledge and power; the latter describes Frankenstein as 'a divine wanderer' (p. 17). They might both be seen as modern, arguably rather selfish, knight errants. The Creature is similarly exiled from normal society due to his appearance and forced to wander across Europe; but by destroying Frankenstein's family, he also turns his creator into a *wrecca*. When Frankenstein has to travel to England for 'two years of exile' (p. 127) in order to create the Creature's bride, he calls himself (yet again) 'a miserable wretch, haunted by a curse that shut up every avenue to enjoyment' (p. 128). And he tells Walton how he has 'traversed a vast portion of the earth' in his quest to avenge himself on the Creature (p. 171). By cursing each other, Frankenstein and the Creature end up cursing themselves, irrevocably separating themselves from society, and making their own lives wretched.

There is perhaps one point in the novel where the bonds between Frankenstein and the Creature are not only those of suffering and hatred. Having launched numerous curses against the Creature on first encountering him ('vile insect', 'wretched devil' and so on), after hearing the Creature's narrative, despite the fact that it includes William's murder, Frankenstein is 'moved' (p. 120). The Creature's plea for companionship sparks a previously latent sense of parental responsibility: 'did I not, as his maker, owe him all the portion of happiness that it was in my power to bestow?' (p. 120). The problem is that despite responding to the Creature's eloquent description of his situation, actually seeing the Creature, 'the filthy mass that moved and talked', destroys his feelings of compassion and replaces them with 'horror and hatred' (p. 121). Furthermore, even if this was not the case, the fact that he is only able to communicate with the Creature after William's murder means that he can never give his creation a sympathetic hearing. Therefore, although he finally agrees to provide the Creature with a mate, this is not due to pity, but because of an abstract, rational calculation about the justice due to the Creature and to humanity as a whole (pp. 121–22). Because Frankenstein is unable to care about the Creature's feelings in the way that a parent should do with regard to those of their child, he is able later in the novel to tear apart the creature's mate without remorse. He may be right to do so in terms of the possible negative consequences, but, again, creating life without nurturing it is at the root of Shelley's concerns.

MORALITY AND DEATH

Early on during his narrative, Frankenstein breaks off to warn the excited Walton that he will not tell him the secret of life:

> I will not lead you on, unguarded and ardent as I then was, to your destruction and infallible misery. Learn from me, if not by my precepts, at least by my example, how dangerous is the acquirement of knowledge, and how much happier that man is who believes his native town to be the world, than he who aspires to become greater than his nature will allow. (p. 35)

This is a very conventional moral: be content with your place in life and do not overreach your capacity. Frankenstein presents himself as the terrible embodiment of what happens if you ignore such 'precepts'. And yet, as I argued in the previous chapter, Walton does ignore them. Furthermore, at times so does Frankenstein himself. There are points in the narrative where he describes himself as having been racked with remorse, emphasizing his responsibility for letting the Creature loose into the world. At other points, though, and particularly during his final days, he refuses to accept any responsibility for the outcome of his endeavours, and this allows at least the possibility that someone else might achieve a different outcome.

The problem, perhaps, is simply that Frankenstein does not believe in the straightforward moral outlined above. This is exemplified in his rousing speech to Walton's crew, who want to turn back should the ice free the ship:

> You were hereafter to be hailed as the benefactors of your species, your name adored, as belonging to brave men who encountered death for honour and the benefit of mankind.

And now, behold, with the first imagination of danger, or, if you will, the first mighty and terrific trial of your courage, you shrink away [. . .]. Oh! be men, or be more than men. [. . .] Do not return to your families with the stigma of disgrace marked on your brows. Return as heroes who have fought and conquered, and who know not what it is to turn their backs on the foe. (p. 183)

Here is the same rhetoric that Frankenstein used to describe his early dreams of scientific glory. The emphasis, again, is on posthumous glory, rather than the benefit of mankind in itself. Frankenstein questions the masculinity of Walton's sailors and threatens them with disgrace. He also sees the natural world, typically, as an enemy to be 'fought and conquered'. And yet there is irony here. Presumably the men's families would prefer that they return marked with 'the stigma of disgrace' than that they did not return at all. To be 'more' than a man may well mean to be a hero; but it can also mean to be a monster. Frankenstein seeks to be more than a man by giving himself the power of a god, and seeks to create a being who is more than a man: bigger, stronger, tougher and so on. As a result, both individuals are outcasts, who achieve no glory and no benefit to humanity. The 'stigma of disgrace', the novel suggests, may be preferable to the stigma of monstrousness.

Frankenstein feels able to give such a stirring exhortation to continue to explore, whatever the risks, because at root he does not believe that his past actions were morally wrong, as he explains to Walton when he is close to death:

During these last days I have been occupied in examining my past conduct; nor do I find it blameable. In a fit of *enthusiastic* madness I created a rational creature, and was bound towards him, to assure, as far as was in my power, his happiness and well-being. This was my duty; but there was another still paramount to that. My duties towards my fellow-creatures had greater claims to my attention, because they included a greater proportion of happiness or misery. Urged by this view, I refused, and I did right in refusing, to create a companion for the first creature. He shewed unparalleled malignity and selfishness, in evil [. . .]. [H]e ought to die. (p. 185; my italics)

Here Frankenstein washes his hands of all responsibility, all guilt, for the Creature's creation and abandonment. He talks about the conflict between private duties – towards what effectively is his offspring – and public duties towards the whole of humanity, and suggests that, using a utilitarian calculus of positive and negative effects, he was right to resist the Creature's entreaty to provide him with a mate. This rationalization of his conduct can only work through a series of problematic omissions and questionable assumptions. As in the earlier stages of his narrative, he suggests that he was mentally ill during the process of creating the Creature, carried away by a fit of 'enthusiasm' that prevented him from thinking rationally about the consequences of his actions. We might wonder, however, whether Frankenstein could not, *or would not*, think about these consequences. Is blaming '*enthusiastic* madness' really a cover for the wilful blindness to consequences created by his egotistical lust for glory?

The discussion of 'duty' is similarly problematic. From the very beginning, Frankenstein neglected his duties to the Creature, effectively abandoning him and letting him unprotected into the world. It could be argued, therefore, that this supposed conflict between private and public duties is the result of this initial failure, and therefore of Frankenstein's own making. To start rationalizing *now* seems perverse, given that his initial response to the Creature, although perfectly understandable, was irrational. Furthermore, we might argue against Frankenstein's utilitarian assumptions. Shelley seems to be alluding here to a famous passage in Godwin's *Political Justice*, in which he had argued that public duties should always outweigh private duties, suggesting that, given the choice between saving the French archbishop Fénelon (the author of what Godwin calls the 'immortal Telemachus') or his valet from a fire, one should always choose Fénelon, even if the valet happened to be one's father (Shelley 1999, pp. 252–54). However, given the novel's emphasis on the importance of domestic affections, we might question whether Shelley would necessarily endorse this view.

Frankenstein also assumes that the creation of a mate for the Creature would have threatened humanity. But would it? Would they have necessarily been able to procreate? Presumably Frankenstein could have made this impossible. And even if they had, would this new 'race' necessarily have threatened mankind? The justification he voices here is a condensed version of the thoughts he describes having had when he is close to finishing the Creature's bride. He fears that she will be 'ten thousand times more malignant' than the Creature, and/or that she will refuse to be the Creature's 'mate', leaving him even more embittered, and/or that they will create a new species that would threaten humanity (p. 138). Again, he presents himself as eventually making a *selfless* decision in a clash between his own benefit (placating the Creature) and that of humanity. Mellor argues that these are false rationalizations concealing Frankenstein's 'fear of female sexuality' and independence (p. 120), which produces a violent assertion of his masculine power: 'trembling with passion, [I] tore the thing to pieces' (p. 139). There is much in this argument, although Mellor's feminist perspective sometimes occludes the novel's ambiguities, particularly with regard to its depiction of Frankenstein. I would certainly not want to argue that he is clearly the villain of the piece. Perhaps it is significant that he does not consider ways in which he might create the bride whilst avoiding the terrible consequences he imagines, but his anxieties about doing so are highly understandable, given all that has happened. The problem is, though, that he never really acknowledges that the Creature's 'malignity' may have been produced by the Creature's unhappy experiences, most notably his abandonment by his 'father'. For Frankenstein, the Creature is innately evil, and his bride is likely to be the same.

Yet, at the same time, Frankenstein still seems fascinated with the idea that someone else may discover the principle of life and create beings who are not 'monstrous'. His final words perfectly encapsulate the contradictions of his position throughout the novel:

Seek happiness in tranquillity, and avoid ambition, even if it be only the apparently innocent one of distinguishing yourself

in science and discoveries. Yet why do I say this? I have myself
been blasted in these hopes, yet another may succeed. (p. 186)

The first sentence gives a similarly conventional moral to the one
he gives towards the start of the narrative, which relates to the
novel's idealization of domestic seclusion and 'tranquillity' and its
critique of the dangers of ambition, exemplified by Frankenstein
and Walton. And yet, at the very end, Frankenstein still hopes that
his discovery of the principle of life may be put to a better use, suggesting, perhaps, that exploration, ambition, and the will to power
are unavoidable aspects of human life. And yet what does he mean
by 'succeed'? After all, he succeeded in creating life. 'Succeed'
might mean to nurture the newly created being and therefore teach
it benevolence, but there is no evidence that Frankenstein believes
that this would have made any difference, and his suggestion that
his hopes have been blasted seems to blame fate or bad luck, rather
than his own behaviour. 'Succeed' seems, for Frankenstein, to
mean to create a being less monstrous, a grateful child (perhaps
one not made out of dismembered corpses) who will be accepted
as part of society. However, as we will see in the following chapter,
given the inequalities that beset humanity, and the human propen-
sity to create 'Others' to fear and despise, this seems like a very
tenuous hope.

CHAPTER 3

CONSTRUCTING A SELF: THE CREATURE'S NARRATIVE

The Creature has to fend for himself right from the beginning, without the nurturing or education provided by parents. By providing such a detailed, first-person account of how a 'filthy mass' of mismatched body parts becomes a *character* through experience, reflection and the learning of language, Shelley is able to ask profound questions about identity. How do our experiences affect who we are and who we will become? To what extent does our identity come from 'within' ourselves, and to what extent is it defined by how others see us? What sort of identities are available to those individuals excluded from 'normal' society? What it is like to feel alienated from one's own self? The novel does not necessarily give definitive answers to any of those questions, but the Creature's narrative may well encourage the reader to draw some rather bleak conclusions.

EARLY LIFE

Shelley's account of the Creature's development draws on (without necessarily endorsing) various philosophical treatments of identity and education, most notably by John Locke (1632–1704) and Jean-Jacques Rousseau (1712–78). During the winter of 1816–17, she and PBS read Locke's *Essay Concerning Human Understanding* (1690) (Shelley 1987, vol. 1, pp. 146–53). According to Locke, an *empiricist* philosopher, the human mind begins life as 'white paper void of all characters, without any *ideas*'. All its ideas come from experience, either from 'SENSATION', that is, perceptions of the world, or from 'REFLECTION', when the mind self-consciously perceives its own operations (Locke 1993, pp. 45–46). Locke's philosophy, then, tended to support the argument that a person's character was created by their experiences, rather than by innate ideas or tendencies that they were born with.

Rousseau was for many years a citizen of Frankenstein's home city of Geneva. As I discussed in the Introduction, he has a pervasive and complex presence in *Frankenstein*. His confessional writings impact on the narrative form and the characters' rhetoric of alienation, and his concern about the relationship between nature and culture is central to the novel. The two key texts with regard to the Creature's narrative are *A Discourse on Inequality* (1755) and *Émile* (1762). The *Discourse* argues that human beings would be happier and more 'authentic' in 'a state of nature'. *Émile* considers how children might best be nurtured and educated to enter society while preserving their natural unspoilt condition, and at one point imagines the confused and imbecilic state of 'a child [who] had at his birth the stature and the strength of a grown man' (Rousseau 1979a, p. 61); like the Creature, such a child would have no more understanding of the world than would a small baby. This is apparent in the opening of the Creature's narrative, which attempts to describe an infantile, pre-linguistic state, in which the blank slate of the mind is bombarded by sensations that are 'confused and indistinct' (p. 79) because they have not been subject to reflection. The Creature describes how he was unable 'to distinguish between the operations of [his] various senses' and how he had 'no distinct ideas'; his mind is an unruly mass of sensory information and basic desires ('hunger' and 'thirst'). There is nothing innately monstrous about the Creature's mind; it follows the normal process of development according to Lockean empiricism. However, it is not a pleasant process, particularly for an abandoned child; unprotected from the cold, he becomes overwhelmed by pain and confusion (p. 80).

As time passes, the Creature becomes able to attach distinct ideas to distinct objects through a process of sensation and thought. And by discovering fire, he moves from a 'pure' state of nature to utilize the most basic technology associated with human culture. Like his creator, the Creature is a scientist, con-ducting experiments to try to improve on his natural existence.[1] Through a process of observation and *reflection*, he learns to dry wood, fan embers and cook food (p. 82). This makes his exis-tence considerably more comfortable, at least for a short time, but lack of food forces him to travel away. As a result, he encounters human civilization for the first time; no longer a solitary 'natural man', he manages to find food and shelter, but now has to deal with other individuals' hostile responses to him, leading to his self-loathing and sense of alienation.

The Creature's biographical trajectory presents in micro-cosm Romantic-period debates about nature versus culture, and encapsulates the novel's ambivalent attitude to both. For Rousseau, the natural man is relatively happy because he is entirely autonomous, self-sufficient (physically and psycho-logically), and lacks the artificial needs created by culture. Although he does feel some sort of innate compassion for others (Rousseau 1984, p. 99), he does not engage in social rela-tionships: 'savage man, wandering in the forest, without work, without speech, and without relationships, was equally without any need of his fellow men and without any desire to hurt them' (Rousseau 1984, p. 104). It is significant that the Creature does not describe himself as feeling lonely during the early stages of his life; this only begins when he encounters the De Lacey family. Rousseau argues that most forms of human unhappiness would have been avoided if humanity had stayed in its natural state. Physical health is related to psychological health; furthermore, 'the state of reflection is a state contrary to nature, and [. . .] the man that meditates is a depraved [corrupt] animal' (p. 85). The worst thing about reflection, for Rousseau, is that it gives rise to what he calls *amour-propre*, a selfish pride born of social inter-action and comparing ourselves to others (p. 114). Again, it is notable that the Creature only becomes psychologically troubled and alienated from himself when he starts to compare himself to the De Laceys and reflects on how they might perceive him. In his conclusion to the *Discourse*, Rousseau contrasts the 'peace and freedom' of the 'savage man' with the state of the 'civil man', who, being always active, sweating, and restless, torments himself endlessly in search of ever more laborious occupations; he works himself to death, he even runs towards the grave to put himself into shape to live, or renounces life in order to gain immortality. (p. 136)

This seems extraordinarily appropriate as a description of Frankenstein, who has a strong sense of *amour-propre* and whose case enacts Rousseau's metaphors. His ardent, painful, laborious activity in pursuit of glory ('immortality') entails a literal running into the grave (!) in order to try to create, improve, and extend life ('immortality' again). However, this only leads to death and 'torment' for himself and his family. Similarly, as the Creature experiences society and reflects on those experiences, he becomes 'restless' in his desire for revenge, leading to the destruction of others and his own self-immolation.

In contrast to Rousseau, numerous writers of the eighteenth century and the Romantic period extolled the benefits of culture and improvement. Humphry Davy, for example, who had such an impact on the representation of science in *Frankenstein*, contrasted the weakness of natural man with the power of science:

Man, in what is called a state of nature, is a creature of almost pure sensation. Called into activity only by positive wants, his life is passed either in satisfying the cravings of the common appetites, or in apathy, or in slumber. [. . .] He has no vivid feelings of hope, or thoughts of permanent and powerful action. And, unable to discover causes, he is either harassed by superstitious dreams, or quietly and passively submitted to the mercy of nature and the elements. How different is man informed through the beneficence of the Deity, by science, and the arts! [. . .] [Science] has bestowed upon him powers that may be almost called creative; which have enabled him to change and modify the beings surrounding him, and by his experiments to interrogate nature with power, not simply as a scholar, passive and seeking only to understand her operations, but rather as a master, active with his own instruments. (Shelley 1999, p. 272)

Critics have discussed this passage in relation to Victor Frankenstein (for example, Mellor 1989, p. 93), but it also applies to the Creature, who moves from a state of 'pure sensation' to develop rudimentary technology, and to experience complex hopes and desires. Unlike Rousseau, Davy sees 'natural man' as inadequate: stupid, weak, and anxious. Through science, however, humanity is able to 'master' the natural world and modify its environment, becoming Godlike in its capacity to *create* (I think Davy uses the phrase '*almost* called creative' because he is trying to avoid seeming to suggest that human beings can mimic or even challenge divine power, even though he effectively does suggest this!). The emphasis on scientific power in the final sentence is perhaps slightly disturbing – one might ask who or what Davy means by 'beings', and whether or not they want to be 'change[d] and modif[ied]'. And what about the responsibility of the scientist to these beings? As the epigraph to the novel asks, quoting *Paradise Lost*, 'Did I request thee, Maker, from my clay / To mould Me man?' (p. 1).

Frankenstein does not idealize the state of nature. The Creature suffers a great deal of pain from hunger, cold and confusion. Fire keeps him warm and makes his food more pleasant; he benefits from the food and shelter at the shepherd's house; and he strongly admires the first village he encounters. But the book does not idealize culture either. Fire can cause pain as well as pleasure (p. 81) and social existence exposes you to the prejudices and selfish interests of others. It can also make you alienated from yourself because you care so much about how others see you. It is fitting, therefore, that the Creature uses the simple technology of fire to destroy the De Laceys' cottage after they have rejected him (p. 113) and to end his own life (p. 191). However, the novel represents culture not as a choice but as an inevitable result of the human capacity to reflect. Individuals will seek to better their condition, they will conduct experiments, and they will reflect on the results. Experience cannot be unlearned, however unfortunate its effects, and that in itself is a natural process: as the Creature puts it, knowledge 'clings to the mind, when it has once seized on it, like a lichen on a rock' (p. 96). Perhaps Frankenstein's creation of life does transgress some sort of natural order, but perhaps that transgression is in itself part of a *natural* process. And, the novel asks, is his desire to prolong life and banish disease really different in kind from the Creature's fanning of the fire to keep away the cold?

EDUCATION

Much critical ink has been spilled in analysing the Creature's learning of language and discussing how the books he reads resonate throughout the novel. In describing the Creature's early engagement with the 'godlike science' of language (p. 88), Shelley again follows Locke, showing words to be arbitrary marks of ideas that have already been 'collected' by experience (Locke 1993, pp. 227–31). Hence, over several months, the Creature is able to recognize simple nouns such as '*fire, milk, bread*, and *wood*' and to discover the De Laceys' names (pp. 88, 89). Through the convenient device of the family teaching French to Safie, the Creature is able to progress quickly in the language. We might find this rapid development rather unconvincing, but it is worth noting that the Creature seems to have superhuman mental powers as well as physical ones.

As a result of this new facility, the Creature is able to learn a great deal simply from listening to the cottagers' conversations. This new knowledge, though, is frequently painful to him. His understanding of family life and the 'mutual bonds' between human beings serves to emphasize his own freakishness and alienation, and leads to unanswered questions about his identity. At the same time, his knowledge of human 'virtues' and 'vices', combined with his observation of the 'benevolence and generosity' of the De Laceys (p. 102), fuels his desire to become part of the human world, a desire that can never be satisfied and is later transformed into a violent hatred of humanity.

The Creature encounters four books while at the De Laceys' cottage, which seem to have been chosen very carefully by Shelley. Felix instructs Safie using Volney's *Ruins of Empires* (1791),[2] and the Creature rather fortuitously finds a 'leathern portmanteau' (p. 103) containing Milton's *Paradise Lost* (1667), 'Plutarch's Lives' (*Parallel Lives*, originally written c. 100 AD) and Goethe's sentimental novel *The Sorrows of Young Werther* (1779 in French and English; originally published in German in 1774 as *Die Leiden des Jungen Werthers*). Volney's book, which had a powerful influence on some Romantic intellectuals, was a radical history of the world that attacked despotism and religion. From it, the Creature learns about empires and their decline, and also about the terrible consequences of exploration and imperialism: 'I heard of the discovery of the American hemisphere, and wept with Safie over the hapless fate of its original inhabitants' (p. 95). Here the Creature is referring to how the native peoples of North and South America were wiped out by the process of colonization. Interestingly, this echoes Victor's remarks to Walton early in his narrative, that if men were content with their 'domestic affections', 'America would have been discovered more gradually; and the empires of Mexico and Peru had not been destroyed' (p. 37). Both Frankenstein and his creation, therefore, voice the novel's critique of the masculine 'will to power', exemplified in the conjunction of science, exploration, and imperialism, although the example of all three major characters suggests that these processes may be very difficult to prevent. Perhaps some people will never be content with 'domestic affections'; and, as the Creature notes with horror, although humanity is 'noble and godlike', it is also 'vicious and base' and capable of 'vice and bloodshed' (p. 96).

Peter Brooks has noted that the three books discovered by the Creature 'cover the public, private, and the cosmic realms, and three modes of love' (Botting 1995a, p. 87). What the Creature ultimately learns from his reading is the extent to which he is *excluded* from all three realms and modes. Plutarch's *Parallel Lives* gives biographies of Greek and Roman 'great men'. Its focus, therefore, is on public life, and the volume read by the Creature deals with figures who (supposedly) founded 'ancient republics' (of the five listed by the Creature, only Solon is a figure of history, rather than of legend). The book inculcates civic virtue (that is, *love* for one's country/state).[3] The private realm and sexual love are the subjects of *The Sorrows of Young Werther*, a highly influential sentimental novel describing how the sensitive and talented protagonist suffers because of his unrequited love for a married woman and ends up committing suicide. The Creature's response to this text is interesting. For modern readers, Werther can sometimes seem self-obsessed, self-dramatizing and self-pitying, but the Creature sees him as 'a more divine being than I had ever beheld or imagined'. He also 'inclines' towards Werther's opinion that suicide can be justified in certain cases, and weeps over his death. In some important ways, Werther's situation is analogous to the Creature's. He is highly self-conscious and sensitive, and unable to 'fit in' to normal society: he cannot be part of bourgeois family life – represented by the marriage of his love Lotte to the sensible Albert – and he is humiliated at court because he is not of sufficiently high social status (Goethe 1989, pp. 80–82). His suicide expresses his separation from society; similarly, the Creature wishes he had killed himself after the De Laceys reject him (p. 110).

Paradise Lost deals with the cosmic realm and divine love. We have already seen that it is important to an understanding of Frankenstein's character. Understandably, the creature compares his situation to that of Adam:

> Like Adam, I was created apparently united by no link to any other being in existence [. . .]. [But] he had come forth from the hands of God a perfect creature, happy and prosperous, guarded by the especial care of his Creator. (p. 105)

This again makes the point about Frankenstein's failure as a 'Creator': lack of care for his *creation* leaves him 'wretched, helpless, and alone', without any connection to other beings. Similarly, the Creature states that:

> no Eve soothed my sorrows, or shared my thoughts. I remembered Adam's supplication to his Creator; but where was mine? he had abandoned me, and, in the bitterness of my heart, I cursed him. (p. 106)

Therefore, at times he identifies himself with Satan, who envied the happiness of Adam and Eve. Like Frankenstein, the Creature recognizes his alienation and emotional suffering as authentically

Satanic: 'I, like the arch fiend, bore a hell within me' (p. 111). Unlike all these characters, though, the Creature's suffering is not brought on by choice: Satan, and Adam and Eve, it could be argued, chose to rebel against God, and therefore brought suffering on to themselves. (Another point of view would be that Eve was not nurtured by God in the same way as Adam and therefore her 'rebellion' was justified.) And, in a sense, the Satan-like Frankenstein rebels against his creation, refusing to acknowledge his responsibility for it. The Creature, on the other hand, wants desperately to 'fit in' with prevailing laws and codes; barred from doing so, he is forced to become a Satanic rebel.

It is important to note the other reading matter that the Creature discovers during this period: Frankenstein's journal describing the Creature's creation. Again, knowledge leads to suffering: the Creature's insight into his 'accursed origin' feeds his self-loathing. In a phrase typical of the novel's self-consciousness about textuality and representation, the Creature tells Victor that the description of him was 'in language which painted your own horrors, and rendered mine ineffaceable' (p. 105). Reading and writing can be liberating, but they can also be constricting. Victor's diary fixes the Creature's identity as 'horrible', and prevents the Creature from ever forgetting ('effacing') this identity. It is through language that the Creature comes to realize his irredeemable monstrousness, although we shall see that it also creates at least the possibility of transcending it.

'OTHERING'

Due to his size and corpse-like appearance, the Creature consistently provokes fear and hostility in every person he encounters. They see him as an inhuman 'Other', biologically and culturally different from them. What makes him particularly horrifying, however, is that his difference includes similarities: he is humanoid in shape and made up of human body parts. As the Creature himself says to Victor, 'My form is a filthy type of yours, more horrid from its very resemblance' (p. 105). He is a walking embodiment of the death and decay from which all organisms will inevitably suffer, but which human culture seeks to repress or control through taboo (not speaking about it) and ritual. What makes the Creature monstrous is partly that he is inhuman, but partly that he reminds people of what they will eventually become. Recent scholarship in the humanities and social sciences has paid a great deal of attention to the ways in which human beings tend to assert their own individuality or membership of a certain group by defining themselves against an 'Other' – perhaps someone from a different social background, or a different ethnic group – who is stigmatized as inferior and/or threatening. The 'Others' constructed or identified by particular individuals or groups often reflect deep-seated anxieties about themselves. On a very basic level, the Creature is horrifying because he represents the terrible reality of death, which human culture does not want to acknowledge. However, he also reflects a range of other cultural anxieties.

The Creature's very first encounter with a human being produces terror and rejection, setting the pattern for all that follow. Victor wakes up following his nightmare about his mother and Elizabeth:

> He held up the curtain of the bed; and his eyes, if eyes they may be called, were fixed on me. His jaws opened, and he muttered some inarticulate sounds, while a grin wrinkled his cheeks. He might have spoken, but I did not *hear*; one hand was stretched out, seemingly to detain me, but I escaped. (pp. 39–40; my italics)

The Creature does not recount this incident himself, and presumably does not remember it, but it exemplifies the way in which human beings perceive him, a horror which is of course particularly poignant given that Frankenstein is the closest thing he has to a parent. The Creature directs his attention to the first person he sees: he seems to want something. He seeks to communicate but is 'inarticulate'. His intentions are unclear, but that he appears to be grinning and that he stretches out his hand to Frankenstein does not suggest malice. He may appear to the reader rather like a young child reaching out for the affection of a parent.

Frankenstein's perspective on the scene, however, tends to give it a different emphasis. For a start, there is a strange doubt about whether the Creature's eyes should be really described as such, presumably because they are unlifelike: 'watery [. . .] [and] almost of the same colour as the dun white sockets in which they were set' (p. 39). This suggests the extent to which the Creature challenges normal biological and ontological (meaning related to being) categories: is he/it *really* alive? Furthermore, these 'eyes' are 'fixed' on Frankenstein, implying some sort of mysterious and disturbing purpose and, perhaps, a desire to control him. Therefore, Frankenstein finds the Creature's grin and attempts to communicate terrifying, and does not attempt to 'hear' him. One might argue that the only character in the novel properly to 'hear' the Creature is the blind man De Lacey. Frankenstein does not perceive the Creature's reaching out as a child seeking a parent's affection, but as a threatening movement that he must escape from. This passage is echoed much later in the novel when Frankenstein sees the Creature *watching* him as he works on creating his mate. He interprets his 'ghastly grin' not as satisfaction at the prospect of a companion, but as signifying 'the utmost extent of malice and treachery' (p. 139). The issue here is not simply that there is a gap between what the Creature may be intending, and how he is interpreted by others. Given his hideous and disgusting appearance, he is *bound* to be interpreted in a negative way, even by the man who created him. This is the bleak core of the novel, and a problem to which there is no easy solution.

The Creature's second encounter with a human being, and seemingly the first one he can recall, comes at least a week after he has left Ingolstadt. Wandering through the countryside in search of food, he enters a cottage belonging to an old man, who flees in terror. The following day he travels to a village, where he produces fear and violence: 'some fled, some attacked me' (p. 83). He escapes, 'grievously bruised', and eventually takes shelter in the hovel that turns out to be attached to the De Laceys' cottage. This early experience of 'the barbarity of man' (p. 84) sets the pattern for his later encounters. He is ultimately rejected by the De Laceys (p. 110) and even when he saves a young girl from drowning, seeking (interestingly) 'to restore animation' to her 'senseless' body, he is shot by 'a rustic' (p. 115). The Creature, supposedly a wild and savage creature, encounters so-called civilization and is treated with savagery. Here, at least, the novel is authentically Rousseauvian. 'Barbarous', of course, is usually contrasted with 'civilized'; the Latin term *barbarus* was applied to those peoples outside the Roman Empire and itself derives from the Greek term *barbaroi*, meaning people unable to speak Greek. At this early stage in the Creature's narrative, his 'Otherness' is a result of his physical distinctiveness and his inarticulacy. However, from his perspective, the villagers, considering him to be an outsider (out-landish), show their own 'barbarity' by not treating such an 'Other' with respect. This confusion of the categories of 'civilized' and 'barbaric' suggests the way in which the novel also confounds the categories of 'human' and 'monstrous': the Creature is capable of behaving humanely, and the human beings are capable of behaving monstrously. This is best encapsulated by Elizabeth's bleak remark after Justine's execution: 'men appear to me as monsters thirsting for each other's blood' (p. 81).

Despite all these encounters, and his desire to revenge himself on humanity, when he encounters William Frankenstein, the Creature still hopes to make him his 'companion and friend', believing him to be 'unprejudiced' and too young 'to have imbibed a horror of deformity' (pp. 116–17). William responds, predictably, with horror, calling him a 'monster', an 'ugly wretch', an 'ogre', and threatening him with his father's punish-ment (p. 117). He refuses to believe that the Creature's intentions could be benevolent: 'you wish to eat me, and tear me to pieces' (p. 117). The Creature throttles William because he is related to his creator and comes from an apparently ideal family unit from which the Creature is excluded. Furthermore, he represents the apparently insoluble problem of 'Othering'. Even this very young and amiable child has been (from the Creature's point of view) perverted by society; his invocation of his father's name and his reference to the fact that he is a 'Syndic' (elite legislator) show that William is already aware of and part of the structures of patriarchal power. If even William sees the Creature as a cul-turally inferior and frightening being, then what hope does he have with the rest of humanity?

This question is also asked by the Creature's experience of the De Laceys. They are the only human beings, apart from Victor, whom the Creature has the opportunity to 'get to know', although as an observer rather than a friend or acquaintance. Originally from France, they comprise the blind father, his son Felix, his daughter Agatha, and Felix's (presumably) future wife, the Arabian Safie, the daughter of 'a Turkish merchant' and 'a Christian Arab' (pp. 98–99). The De Laceys are a rather idealized family of beautiful and benevolent beings who have undergone a great deal of suffering and dislocation, but have survived through poverty and unhappiness due to strong bonds of affection. When the Creature first encounters them, they are despondent due to Safie's absence and their impoverished situation, but they still treat each other with gentleness and 'kindness and affection' (p. 85). By watching their interactions, the Creature, who previously has felt only basic 'pain and pleasure', begins to experience more complex emotions (p. 85). Through long observation, and from the fact that he performs unseen various domestic tasks for them, the Creature begins to feel part of the family unit, sympathizing with their joys and suffering (p. 89).

The story of the De Laceys, as summarized by the Creature, does not need retelling here in any detail (pp. 98–102). Its importance to the narrative is that it emphasizes certain characteristics of the family. They were once high-ranking and affluent, but have been brought low by Felix's attempt to save Safie's father from unjust imprisonment. As a result, the family were imprisoned and then exiled into poverty. Safie eventually is able to join them, having escaped from her tyrannical and treacherous father.[4] This has a profound effect on the whole family: despite their poverty, they are now able to be 'contented and happy' in their quiet loving existence. The Creature is 'in love' with this familial idyll and imagines that he might become part of it (p. 91). The De Laceys are exemplary individuals; despite all that they have suffered, there is no bitterness or discord between them. Felix's aid of Safie's father shows that they have sympathy for the oppressed, even if from a different background from their own. And the place of Safie in the family suggests at least a certain capacity to accept and, as it were, assimilate 'Otherness', although it is worth noting that Safie may be exotic, but she is also Christian and not necessarily racially different from the De Laceys ('her complexion wondrously fair' (p. 93)). These aspects of the family, along with De Lacey's blindness, make the Creature's fantasy of acceptance a plausible one. If any human beings could tolerate him, it would be the De Laceys. After all, they seem to exemplify the old man's claim that 'the hearts of men [. . .] are full of brotherly love and charity' (p. 109). But like everyone else, they look upon him with horror and react with fear and violence. Their rejection of him is not surprising but it is important, confirming his irredeemable 'Otherness' and alienation.

Our sympathies for much of this narrative are likely to be with the Creature; after all, we do not see his appearance but read his eloquent account of his sufferings. Like the blind De Lacey, we can listen properly to him because we are not *faced* with him. However, that the other characters' responses are understandable is made apparent by the Creature's own reaction when he sees himself for the first time during the period in which he is 'living with' the De Laceys:

> I had admired the perfect forms of my cottagers [. . .]: but how was I terrified, when I viewed myself in a transparent pool! At first I started back, unable to believe that it was indeed I who was reflected in the mirror; and when I became fully convinced that I was in reality the monster that I am, I was filled with the bitterest sensations of despondence and mortification. (p. 90)[5]

The Creature's initial response to his own reflection is fear, followed by a disconnection between his sense of his own essential identity and the image he sees; his self, as it were, becomes split. When he accepts that the reflection accurately depicts his appearance, his notion of his essential identity changes: he begins to see himself as wholly monstrous, endorsing the views of all the human beings he has encountered. His *reflection* on his reflection, while healing the breach between his original idea of himself and his appearance, initially leads to severe sadness and shame and eventually to hatred towards himself and humanity. This is a Rousseauvian moment in that thinking about his identity leads the Creature to experience *amour-propre* and alienation. 'Mortification', interestingly, derives from the Old French *mortifier* ('to cause to die') and is often associated with the decay and wasting of flesh. The Creature's deathly appearance destroys his fantasies of being accepted by his surrogate family: his hopes vanish 'when I beheld my person reflected in water, or my shadow in the moon-shine' (p. 106). Furthermore, the mortification of his fantasy life leads to the physical death of the people he murders.

In an influential essay, the French psychoanalyst Jacques Lacan (1901–81), whose work has had a profound impact on literary studies, discusses the moment when a very young child is able to recognize its own reflection in the mirror.[6] Initially, the child 'jubilantly' identifies with the wholeness of this image, which Lacan calls the 'Ideal-I' (p. 2). Over time, however, the child has to learn that the wholeness of the image is a *fiction* that his or her ego (self) will never be able to attain. This process is necessary so that the child can become a social being and enter what Lacan calls the 'Symbolic Order' of language. Although the Creature's reflection is certainly not an 'Ideal-I' in a positive sense, the 'Monster-I' that he sees does offer him a way of thinking about himself in terms of *wholeness*, however horrific. It is notable that this moment comes directly after a paragraph when he first becomes aware of the existence of human language and begins to try to master it, hoping that he can use such mastery to make the De Laceys 'overlook the deformity of [his] figure' (p. 90). The close proximity of his complete identification with his reflected image to the start of his entry into the 'Symbolic Order' of language suggests a possible solution to the problem of monstrousness. Through language, the monstrous 'Other' is potentially able to overcome the horror of his reflection, to enter society, and to express his desires and needs to others. In a sense, he thereby becomes less 'whole', but this actually empowers his ego because he is no longer completely defined by his monstrous appearance. However, as we know, the Creature's eloquent expression of his needs is not enough to convince anyone to meet them. Although for a time it seems that Frankenstein will do so by creating him a bride, when that ends in disaster, the 'Symbolic Order' of language seems to have failed the Creature. Thus the 'Monster-I' reflected in the pool once more becomes definitive as a description of his identity, both in terms of how others see him, and how he sees himself.

There has been a great deal of critical interest in how the figure of the Creature symbolizes, or at least registers, what we might call cultural and racial 'Others': the beings and groups that bourgeois society of early nineteenth-century Europe sought to define itself against. Many critics have noted how the Creature's weak and marginal position in society can be read in relationship to that of women in a patriarchal culture. In a classic reading of *Frankenstein* in relationship to *Paradise Lost*, Gilbert and Gubar discuss how the portrayal of the Creature exemplifies how Milton, and the patriarchy he represents, see women as monstrous and destructive: Eve, after all, was supposedly seduced by Satan into disobeying God, thereby bringing Sin into the world and causing the expulsion of humanity from Eden (pp. 214–47). Shelley was heavily influenced by, particularly the writings of her mother, Mary Wollstonecraft, *A Vindication of the Rights of Woman*, which criticized the ways in which society marginalized women and attacked ideas about female education in the work of Rousseau and others.[7] These issues were personal as well as political: it has often been argued that the struggles of the Creature echo Shelley's own life history, particularly the death of her mother and her complex relationship with her father (see, for example, the essays by Ellen Moers and U. C. Knoepflmacher in Levine and Knoepflmacher 1979). Furthermore, given the intense social and cultural pressures on women writers during the nineteenth century, the Creature might also be seen to represent Shelley's anxieties about authorship (Poovey 1980; see also Mellor 1989, Morton 2002, pp. 109–11 and Stephen Behrendt's essay in Feldman and Kelley 1995, pp. 69–87).

Several writers have seen the Creature as exemplifying fears of revolution: embodying mob violence and/or the urban proletariat (workers).[8] It is interesting that Frankenstein creates the Creature at Ingolstadt, a place that Shelley would have known about through the writings of the conservative priest Abbé Augustin Barruel, who represented Ingolstadt as having been a hotbed of radicalism, where a secret society of Illuminati conspired to rebel against society and ultimately, as he put it, 'engendered that disastrous monster called Jacobin' (Levine and Knoepflmacher 1979, p. 156; see also Randel 2003, pp. 466–67). The Jacobins were a powerful faction during the French Revolution who, led by Robespierre, controlled France during the period of the Terror. Several scholars, most notably Chris Baldick, have shown how the rhetoric of monstrousness played an important role in British discussions of the French Revolution during the 1790s, with writers like Edmund Burke representing Revolutionary France as a 'monster of a state' and the Jacobins as monstrous cannibals (Baldick 1990, pp. 16–29).

If the portrayal of the Creature can be related to middle-class fears about 'the mob', it also registers sympathy for the poor and oppressed. The Creature himself identifies with them when, by listening in on Felix's lessons to Safie, he learns of 'the strange system of human society':

> I heard of the division of property, of immense wealth and squalid poverty; of rank, descent, and noble blood. [. . .] I learned that the possessions most esteemed by your fellow-creatures were, high and unsullied descent united with riches. [. . .] Without either [a human being] was considered, except in very rare instances, as a vagabond and a slave, doomed to waste his powers for the profit of the chosen few. And what was I? Of my creation and creator I was absolutely ignorant; but I knew that I possessed no money, no friends, no kind of property. I was, besides, endowed with a figure hideously deformed and loathsome; I was not even of the same nature as man. (p. 96)

The Creature has no family status and he lacks wealth or property; thus even if he was human he would be powerless and subject to exploitation by the few. The passage's critique of an unequal society suggests a radical, or at least a reformist, perspective and coheres with the novel's dedication to Godwin. A key issue here is the relationship in this passage between class and biology. Does the Creature's biological difference simply reflect, as some critics seem to believe, the class inequalities that form the basic concerns of the novel? Or is it rather that the Creature's sense of his lowly status is produced by his more fundamental sense that he is innately biologically different from human beings?

The obvious way to try to relate biology and inequality in the novel is to think about race. Shelley was writing at a time during which concepts of racial difference were hotly debated against a background of imperial and colonial expansion, and the abolition of the British slave trade in 1807. Several critics have discussed the Creature as a racial 'Other'. H. L. Malchow suggests that Shelley's portrayal 'drew upon contemporary attitudes towards non-whites, in particular on fears and hopes of the abolition of slavery in the West Indies' (p. 90). As he argues, Shelley would have come across plenty of representations of blacks in public discourse, and she and PBS had read Mungo Park's *Travels in the Interior Districts of Africa* (1799) in 1814 and Bryan Edwards's *History, Civil and Commercial, of the British Colonies in the West Indies* (1793) in the winter of 1814–15 (pp. 99–100). Malchow explores an interesting range of parallels between the characteristics of the Creature and those stereotypically ascribed to black Africans in early nineteenth-century writing on race, such as size, strength, agility, hideousness, savagery and dangerous sexuality. Furthermore, Debbie Lee has recently argued that the 'troubling relationship' that the novel sets up between 'consumption and monstrosity', particularly with reference to cannibalism, 'calls attention' to these issues in early nineteenth-century discussions of slavery and race (2002, pp. 182–84). Given that slavery was such a powerful and emotive issue in the period – it continued in British colonies until the 1830s – it seems perfectly likely that it informed Shelley's conception of the Creature. However, this is not to suggest that this is a novel 'about' slavery and clearly the Creature is not simply a symbol of black African slaves. As Malchow concedes, he has 'yellow skin' (p. 39), and for Joseph Lew, this skin, barely covering the Creature's 'muscles and arteries', relates to the novel's concern with Orientalism by physically linking him to the famine-stricken inhabitants of British-controlled Bengal in India (Lew 1991, p. 273).

Anne K. Mellor, who is perhaps unfairly dismissive of Malchow's claims, has argued instead that in appearance the Creature is much closer to the 'Mongolian race' as classified by the anthropologist Johann Friedrich Blumenbach in 1795, and also expounded by the Shelleys' friend William Lawrence (Heringman 2003, pp. 174–80). There is some decent textual evidence for this reading. Walton sees the Creature from afar before encountering Victor, and describes him as a figure of 'gigantic stature' who seems 'a savage inhabitant of some undiscovered island' (pp. 12, 13). Given the geographical location of Walton's ship north of Archangel, 'the northernmost city in western Asia' and that Frankenstein pursues the Creature 'amidst the wilds of Tartary and Russia' (Heringman 2003, p. 174), the appropriate racial type for a 'savage inhabitant' would be, in early nineteenth-century terms, a 'Mongol'. Mellor concludes by arguing that Shelley does not necessarily endorse ideas of racial inferiority or degeneration, but 'may be suggesting that racial difference and interracial mating are social evils *only* when we see and write them as evil' (Heringman 2003, p. 193). She thinks that *Frankenstein* and Shelley's later novel *The Last Man* imply the importance of embracing 'the racial other': 'If Victor had been able to see his gigantic yellow-skinned Creature as a member of the Family of Man, if he had been able to provide him with the domestic affection he craved [. . .] then he might indeed have produced a more highly evolved variety of the human species – one capable of advancing rather than destroying human civilisation' (Heringman 2003, pp. 193–94). While Mellor's placing of *Frankenstein* within the context of racial theory is suggestive, I am not fully convinced by her conclusions. First, her argument partly depends on the claim that Frankenstein tears up the female Creature because of his horror that she might mate with men. This is possible, but he does not actually give this as a reason: he is concerned that the female might turn 'to the superior beauty of man' because that would lead the Creature to want to take revenge on humanity once again (p. 138). Perhaps more importantly, Mellor makes it sound like the novel ultimately has a simple liberal message: embrace difference. But *Frankenstein* seems to me to focus much more on the terrible difficulties that culture has in accepting anyone or anything that does not fit in with its categories and values. The novel is unremittingly bleak in its depiction of how even the best and most tolerant individuals cannot overcome their horror at the sight of the Creature. This is not to say that Mary Shelley subscribed to nineteenth-century racial hierarchies, but this is a book about the problem of 'Otherness', not its solution.

The critical arguments that I have discussed in this section are all important, but I find some of them overly schematic. A danger of the historicist methodology which is prevalent in literary studies is that it can encourage a sort of competitive context hunting, in which each critic seeks to trump the previous one by finding a new text, event, or discourse that explains what is *really* going on in the primary text that they are discussing. (A slightly different danger is that the many possible contextual readings pile up on one another, obscuring and crushing the text beneath.) But what makes literary texts fascinating is precisely their resistance to this sort of collapse into context. It seems entirely likely that con-temporaneous racial discourse informed Shelley's novel, but to say that the Creature represents 'the Negro', or 'the Mongolian' (or, for that matter, oppressed women, or the revolutionary prole-tariat), is to do the novel a disservice. The figure of the Creature may, or may not be, informed by some or all of these 'Others' of European patriarchal society, but it is not reducible to them.

I suggest above that *Frankenstein* challenges the categories of 'human' and 'monstrous' and in the previous chapter I discuss some of the links between Frankenstein and the Creature. What makes it so difficult to embrace the 'Other' is that it can mean embracing one's fears and anxieties about oneself. This point may need some clarification and for this I turn to the opening page of Rousseau's *Émile*:

> Everything is good as it leaves the hands of the Author of things; everything degenerates in the hands of man. He forces one soil to nourish the products of another. He mixes and con-fuses the climates, the elements, the seasons. [. . .] He turns

everything upside down; he disfigures everything; he loves deformity, monsters. He wants nothing as nature made it, not even man [. . .].

[. . .] In the present state of things a man abandoned to himself in the midst of other men from birth would be the most disfigured of all. Prejudices, authority, necessity, example, all the social institutions in which we find ourselves submerged would stifle nature in him and put nothing in its place. Nature there would be like a shrub that chance had caused to be born in the middle of a path and that the passers-by soon cause to perish by bumping into it from all sides and bending it in every direction. (Rousseau 1979a, p. 37)

An extended discussion of this passage in relationship to *Frankenstein* can be found in Lawrence Lipking's fine essay on the novel (Shelley 1996b, pp. 322–30).[9] Here I will focus on a few key points. Human beings, for Rousseau, corrupt the natural environment and natural ways of behaving. Frankenstein's desire to improve the natural human being exemplifies this in the stark-est possible way: as Rousseau puts it, 'not even man' is free of humanity's meddling. Human culture, then, is monstrous because it is contrary to nature, and it corrupts and perverts nature when it encounters it. We do not have to believe that *Frankenstein* is necessarily endorsing this view, but it is very clearly addressing it. Rousseau is partly talking about technology here, but he talking more broadly about culture and particularly 'social institutions'. One reading of the novel is simply that such institutions (family, community, the law) *respond* to the Creature's 'Otherness' by excluding it. However, we might think about the ways in which they *construct* the Creature as 'Other'. The Creature can be seen as 'literalizing' Rousseau's metaphor of disfigurement. Supposedly unnatural, he is in fact far closer to 'nature' than anyone else he encounters. Like Rousseau's 'shrub', though, he is beset by 'prejudices' to the extent that his natural benevolence is 'stifle[d]' and he is made *monstrous*. The Creature hopes to reverse, or at least freeze, this process, by getting Frankenstein to make him a bride, who will provide him with the unprejudiced companionship he craves. He imagines that they will be able to escape from civilization into something like a Rousseauvian state of nature (compare Rousseau 1984, p. 81):

> I will go to the vast wilds of South America. My food is not that of man; I do not destroy the lamb and the kid, to glut my appetite; acorns and berries afford me sufficient nourishment. My companion will be of the same nature as myself, and will be content with the same fare. We shall make our bed of dried leaves; the sun will shine on us as on man, and will ripen our food. The picture I present to you is peaceful and human [. . .] (p. 120; my italics)

The future that the Creature envisages for himself and his companion is natural, simple, completely peaceful (even vegetarian), and more authentically *human* than any form of social organization. One might argue that it is simply society's prejudices – exemplified by Victor's eventual refusal to create a companion for the Creature – that prevent this idyll from happening. But perhaps a more interesting reading would be to think about the way in which the Creature's idyll, like all such idylls, is revealed to be a fantasy. Even Rousseau admitted that the 'state of nature' may never have really existed (Rousseau 1984, p. 78).

THE CREATURE, FRANKENSTEIN AND WALTON

In the previous chapters, I have discussed strong links and parallels between Walton, Frankenstein and the Creature. I want to finish this chapter by thinking some more about the Creature's relationship with the two men. Apart from the blind De Lacey, they are the only people in the world with whom he manages to communicate. In their discussions, the Creature eloquently argues his case, but invariably struggles to elicit their understanding or sympathy. This is, as one would expect, partly because of his disgusting appearance. Even Walton, to whom the appearance of the Creature should be considerably less of a shock than it is to anyone other than Frankenstein, is so appalled by his 'loathsome [. . .] hideousness' that he closes his eyes 'involuntarily' (p. 187). It is also, of course, because they see him as morally monstrous due the murders he has committed. To some extent, the Creature ends up concurring with their view of him, but he also has a sense that he has been treated unjustly by society and particularly by Frankenstein. This means that his attitude to his creator can seem paradoxical:

> Unfeeling, heartless creator! you had endowed me with perceptions and passions, and then cast me abroad an object for the scorn and horror of mankind. But on you only had I any claim for pity and redress [. . .] (p. 114)

If Frankenstein really is unfeeling and heartless, then the demand for 'pity' will be a pointless one. But the Creature's expostulation is really a rhetorical ploy to try to make Frankenstein feel guilty and to elicit his sympathy. He wants his creator to move from his past 'pitiless' behaviour to looking on his creation with 'compassion' (p. 120). We saw in Chapter 1 how strongly Walton desires a friend who can sympathize with him and share his feelings. The Creature's needs are the same, but even more pressing. He wants a mate so that there can be what he calls 'the interchange of those sympathies necessary for my being' (p. 118). This is an important phrase. 'Interchange' means a reciprocal exchange: that is, the Creature will be able imagine and feel how his companion is feeling, and vice versa. Such an exchange is 'necessary'; the Creature cannot imagine himself as continuing to exist without a similar being to engage with. This can be compared interestingly to Walton's arguably more narcissistic desire for a friend who would sympathize with *his* emotions (p. 8).

Frankenstein's destruction of the Creature's companion means that there can be no such interchange: the Creature's affections will be unrequited (p. 140). During the rest of the novel, the Creature seeks to make up for this lack with a different sort of interchange: one of hatred and vengeance. By killing off Frankenstein's family, he becomes the only individual to whom Victor has a close bond. At the same time, their previous roles are reversed. The Creature is like a son who becomes stronger than his father. Victor becomes dependent on him as he pursues the Creature across Europe and Asia. Frankenstein imagines that the food he finds during moments when he is overcome by hunger was set there by some sort of providence, 'a spirit of good'. But given that the Creature also supplies him with guidance and sustenance during the pursuit (p. 174), this 'spirit' seems like the fantasy of an exhausted traveller. It also alludes to the period when the Creature performs 'invisible' labours for the De Laceys, which they put down to the actions of a 'good spirit' (p. 91). The Creature has finally succeeded in inextricably linking himself to a human being.

Both characters need each other because there is no one else for them to turn to. There is an interchange here, although one of antipathies rather than sympathies. Given that this is the only interchange the Creature will ever have, it is not surprising that he wishes to die after Frankenstein's death, for he no longer has an 'other' through which to define his own 'self': as he says to Walton, 'I have devoted my creator, the select specimen of all that is worthy of love and admiration among men, to misery [. . .]. You hate me; but your abhorrence cannot equal that with which I regard myself' (p. 190). We may not be convinced that Frankenstein is uncomplicatedly the 'select specimen' that the Creature describes. Perhaps this is an idealized version of him that reflects the Creature's guilt at 'rebelling' against his father. On the other hand, we might see it as a powerful piece of evidence suggesting that the novel is not necessarily giving a straightforward critique of the male imagination through its depiction of Frankenstein. Even the Creature recognizes his benevolence and worth. And yet, once again, our sympathies as readers are much more likely to be with the Creature because we are not faced with his disgusting appearance. When he tells Walton, rather beautifully, that 'I shall no longer see the sun or stars, or feel the winds play on my cheeks. Light, feeling, and sense, will pass away' (p. 190), we are reminded of his vulnerable, infantile state at the beginning of his narrative, when all his senses were confused and he had to learn to distinguish different natural phenomena. With his discovery of fire he began his long, agonizing journey into the corrupt heart of human culture, and it is only through one final conflagration that he can return to the peace and purity of nature, even if he will no longer be able to experience it.

CONCLUSION

This book does not seek to give a definitive account of *Frankenstein*. Inevitably, my focus on characterization means that some formal aspects of the novel – for example, its plotting, or the frame narrative – have not been discussed in great detail, although I have tried to draw your attention to such things. I have explored those themes and contexts that seem to me to be important and interesting, but there are certainly areas of the text that I could have emphasized further. You may feel, perhaps, that there is much more to say about the novel's treatment of gender difference, including the influence of Mary Wollstonecraft. I might have given greater consideration to those passages in which characters experience the sublimity of nature. I have noted the issues of reading, writing and textuality raised by this novel, but have not engaged in an extended discussion of them. Furthermore, you might well disagree with some of my arguments; for instance, my claim that the portrayal of Victor Frankenstein is highly ambivalent. This is all well and good. I would hate to think of this book as writing itself on to the blank paper of its readers' minds. Rather, I would like to imagine students *engaging* with it and using it to help them formulate *their own* responses to this fascinating novel. As I mentioned in the introduction, an enormous amount has been written on *Frankenstein*, and I would also like to imagine that (if nothing else) this book will have drawn your attention to some of the best and stimulating criticism, from which I myself have learnt a great deal.

There is nothing intellectually unsatisfactory about discussing a novel's characters, but we must always remember that they are literary devices, not real people, and that there may be more interesting things to say about a text than what we think of the individuals it depicts. By this stage it should be clear how an analysis of *Frankenstein*'s characters leads us to think about the various issues that the novel is exploring. In Chapter 1, we examined the numerous parallels between Walton and Frankenstein in relationship to some of the novel's key areas of interest: the imagination (and poetry), exploration, science and empire, and the links between them. I emphasized the importance of the frame narrative, and the fact that we hear about the novel's events through Walton's perspective. Chapter 2 argued for the complexity and ambivalence of the representation of Frankenstein: he is much more than the irresponsible mad scientist of myth. However, I also suggested that the novel registers a distrust of the violent, arguably masculine, urge to 'interrogate' the universe. We also thought about *Frankenstein*'s treatment of domestic affections: on the one hand, they are idealized; on the other, there may be the implication that the incestuous closeness of Frankenstein's family stimulates his aberrant behaviour. The close links and parallels between Frankenstein and his creation were also considered. Chapter 3 focused on the Creature's experience of the world, his education and his encounters with a hostile society. The Rousseauvian celebration of the 'state of nature' and denigration of culture are important here, but I suggested that the novel is not uncritically endorsing these views. We thought about how language offers a possible escape from 'Otherness', and how the portrayal of the Creature may be informed by the various 'Others' of early nineteenth-century European culture. I concluded by considering how the Creature replaces Frankenstein's family.

There are many reasons why we should find *Frankenstein* intellectually interesting, but perhaps the principal one is that it asks fundamental questions about human life. Such questions may be answered, and perhaps formulated, very differently in the twenty-first century compared to 1818, but they are still at root the same questions. To what extent are we responsible for our actions? To what extent is technology a blessing, and to what extent is it a curse? Is nature preferable to culture? What makes us human, and how can we avoid becoming monsters? *Frankenstein*, though, refuses to give definitive answers to these questions, or even at times to stick to the categories on which they are based. It is certainly not a didactic piece of writing. Even if it does criticize the human urge to conquer the universe, and society's mistreatment of those individuals that cannot easily be assimilated into its categories, it also shows an understanding of why these processes might occur. Perhaps it would have been better if Walton and Frankenstein had stayed at home with their families, but escaping from the family unit and sublimating affection and sexuality into ambition can be a necessary stage in a person's development, and can have positive as well as negative consequences for society as a whole. (Although the fact that I believe this may say rather too much about me, and the extent to which I've been conditioned by a liberal individualist ideology!) The novel's tragic events would have been avoided if the De Laceys had clasped the Creature to their bosoms, but human beings are sometimes unable to relate to those who seem very different from themselves. All social structures, including the bourgeois family, are defined by what they *exclude*.

There is, of course, a pleasure in contemplating fictional horrors, but this text seeks to challenge its readers as well as to entertain them. Its view of human society is in my opinion rather bleak, and it consistently suggests that 'human' and 'monster' are highly unstable and subjective categories (as the strong links and rhetorical slippage between Frankenstein and his creation reveal). In a stimulating essay, Lawrence Lipking has pointed out the modern tendency to sympathize with the Creature and to denigrate Victor Frankenstein (Shelley 1996b, pp. 313–31). This is a text about interpretation and misinterpretation, and which invites the reader into making certain misreadings because he or she is not faced with the Creature's 'Otherness'. Walton and Frankenstein have their own peculiar perspectives, of course, but so do we. We never have to deal with the Creature's monstrousness, moral or physical, and in his eloquent account of sufferings, we forget that he is a child murderer. There is a sense in which we might be made monstrous by those sympathies, again challenging the fixed categories of 'human' and 'monster'. As readers of a work of Gothic fiction, carried by the violent logic of the plot, we might actually *want* William, Justine and Clerval to die, so that we can enjoy the events that unfold. Caught up in our readerly enthusiasm, we revel (like Frankenstein himself) in images of putrefaction and scenes of transgression. In the novel's opening sentence, Walton notes his sister's 'evil forebodings' about his 'enterprise' and tells her that she 'will rejoice to hear that no disaster' has occurred (p. 5). We, the other absent interlocutors of the explorer's narrative, also have 'evil forebodings' and rejoice when the novel fulfils them. Like the human monsters depicted by Elizabeth after Justine's execution, we thirst for blood.

CHARACTERIZATION IN THE 1831 EDITION

Shelley made some moderately significant revisions to the 1831 edition of *Frankenstein*. This appendix focuses on their effects on characterization, but if you are writing on *Frankenstein* it is well worth thinking more generally about the differences between the two editions. A full list of textual variants can be found in Nora Crook's edition of the novel (Shelley 1996a, pp. 182–227). Marilyn Butler helpfully summarizes and lists the 'substantive variants' in Appendix B to her edition of the 1818 text. As I noted in the Introduction, critics disagree about which edition is to be preferred. There is little doubt that the revised version is more stylistically polished. However, Butler and others have argued that it is also more conservative, downplaying the radical science of the 1818 version and offering a more Christianized worldview.

The revisions have no real impact on the Creature's characterization, but Butler suggests that the characters of Walton and Frankenstein are 'softened, made more sympathetic and admirable' (p. 198). Frankenstein does seem a little more remorseful than in the 1818 text, and Walton places even more emphasis on his virtues: 'the extraordinary merits of this wonderful man' (p. 203). He is also given 'an explicitly religious consciousness' (p. 199). There is generally a stronger sense that he was led by fate to create the monster, rather than by his own free will. His 'guardian angel' initially manages to draw him away from natural philosophy (p. 211), but 'the Angel of Destruction' leads him to Ingolstadt, where he is corrupted by the teachings of Krempe and Waldman (p. 213). As he listens to the latter's inspiring discourse, described as 'the words of fate', Frankenstein feels as if his soul 'were grappling with a palpable enemy', suggesting the temptations of the Devil (p. 213).

I am not so sure that Walton is more 'admirable', but perhaps he does learn more from Frankenstein's narrative than he does in the 1818 version. Early on, the 1831 text places even more emphasis on the explorer's obsessional desire for knowledge and power. Referring mainly (although perhaps not entirely) to his own existence, he tells Frankenstein that 'one man's life or death were but a small price to pay for the dominion I should acquire over the elemental foes of our race' (p. 202). This prompts Frankenstein to tell his story more explicitly than in the 1818 edition as a *warning*: 'Do you share my madness?' (p. 202). He hopes that Walton will derive an 'apt moral' from it (p. 203), although ultimately Frankenstein is still ambivalent about what this moral might be. Having heard this story, and while trapped in the ice, Walton expresses a concern for his crew that is not apparent in the 1818 text: 'it is terrible to reflect that the lives of all these men are endangered through me. If we are lost, my mad schemes are the cause' (p. 228).

With regard to Frankenstein's family, it is notable that Elizabeth is no longer related to him (p. 206), thus there is no longer the suggestion of incest. The beauty and nobility of Clerval and Elizabeth are emphasized even more than in the original edition. Perhaps the most important addition relates to Clerval. The 1831 edition strongly links him 'to Walton's ambitions and to British trade and empire-building in India' (Lew 1991, p. 263). His childhood reading now includes stories of the Crusades against the Islamic 'infidels' (p. 208). And he visits England with Frankenstein because he wishes to be involved in the imperial project:

His design was to visit India, in the belief that he had in his knowledge of its various languages, and in the views he had taken of its various languages, and in the views he had taken of its society, the means of materially assisting the progress of European colonisation and trade. In Britain only could he further the execution of his plan. (p. 225)

Thus the sensitive and imaginative Clerval is linked to the exploration, colonization and exploitation that the Creature weeps over with Safie (p. 95) and that Frankenstein laments (p. 37). Clerval the scholar, like Walton the explorer and Frankenstein the scientist, cannot be content with 'domestic affections' (p. 37) and seeks to turn his knowledge into power, whatever the consequences.

NOTES

INTRODUCTION: AN OVERVIEW OF *FRANKENSTEIN*

1. Sir Walter Scott, in his 1818 review of *Frankenstein*, places it in 'the class of marvellous romances' (Morton 2002, p. 41).
2. Greer's view might carry more weight if her article did not contain basic errors and misunderstandings. To take a couple of examples (there are others), not only does she get Walton's first name wrong, but she complains that the 'inarticulate' Creature speaks in paragraphs. Given that his story (as told by Frankenstein) is transcribed by Walton, it would be bizarre if his speech *did not* appear in paragraphs.
3. For some interesting remarks on *Frankenstein*'s style, see Stephen Behrendt's essay 'Language and Style in *Frankenstein*', in Behrendt 1990, pp. 77–84.
4. Please note that, mainly for the sake of convenience, throughout this book I generally refer to Mary Wollstonecraft Godwin/Shelley as Shelley. Her husband from 1816, Percy Bysshe Shelley, is referred to by the initials PBS.
5. For an interesting biographical reading of *Frankenstein*, which focuses on Shelley's relationship with Godwin, see U. C. Knoepflmacher's essay 'Thoughts on the Aggression of Daughters', in Levine and Knoepflmacher 1979, pp. 88–119.
6. For a full discussion of the vitalist controversy, see Ruston 2005.
7. The ghost story competition also produced Byron's *A Fragment* (1819), Polidori's *The Vampyre: A Tale* (1819), which was based on Byron's unfinished story and published in the *New Monthly Magazine* as Byron's work, and Polidori's novel *Ernestus Berchtold; or, The Modern Oedipus* (1819). Shelley's account of *Frankenstein*'s conception is challenged and compared to evidence in Polidori's diary in Rieger 1963.
8. For anyone interested in the composition of *Frankenstein*, Charles E. Robinson's excellent edition of *The 'Frankenstein' Notebooks* is indispensable (Shelley 1996c).

9. For a more detailed account of Frankenstein's composition, publication, and early reception, see Shelley 1996a, pp. xciii–ci. Extracts from Sir Walter Scott's review in *Blackwood's Edinburgh Magazine* and PBS's 1818 essay on the novel can be found in Morton 2002.
10. A full list of variants between the three editions can be found in Shelley 1996a, pp. 182–227.

CHAPTER 1: WALTON THE EXPLORER

1. There is an interesting parallel here with Daniel Defoe's influential novel of exploration and colonization *Robinson Crusoe* (1719). Crusoe's father commands him not to go to sea, to be content with being born into the 'middle station' of life, and to avoid ambition and adventure (Defoe 2003, p. 6). As with Frankenstein and Walton, ignoring the demands of family leads the explorer into considerable danger and hardship.
2. For a full account of the relationship between 'enthusiasm' and Romantic poetics, see Mee 2003.
3. For Shelley's reading of tales of exploration, see Beck 2000, p. 23; Fulford *et al.* 2004, p. 170; Richard 2003, p. 297; and Shelley 1996a, p. 10.
4. Richard 2003 convincingly places *Frankenstein* in the context of Romantic-period polar exploration, and suggests that Shelley is offering a critique of the enterprise.
5. For a detailed account of polar exploration and theories of magnetism in the Romantic period, which I have drawn on in this paragraph, see Fulford *et al.* 2004, chapter 7.
6. Maurice Hindle suggests that the scientist Humphry Davy, whose writings influenced *Frankenstein*, believed that electricity might be created at the poles (Shelley 1992, p. xxxii).
7. For discussions of these issues in relation to Walton's narrative, see Chantler 1999 and Newman 1986.
8. Favret writes interestingly on the genre of *Frankenstein* and how its epistolary form collapses: see Favret 1993, Chapter 6.
9. In his excellent essay 'Fire and Ice in *Frankenstein*', Griffin argues that both Walton and Frankenstein, as Romantic visionaries, desire to reconcile these apparent opposites (Levine and Knoepflmacher 1979, pp. 49–73).

CHAPTER 2: FRANKENSTEIN THE SCIENTIST

1. For a discussion of how some recent plays have reflected on modern anxieties about science in relationship to the Romantic period, see my essay 'Theatre and Science', in Holdsworth and Luckhurst 2007.

2. For some interesting thoughts on the significance of Geneva to the novel as a whole, see Randel 2003, pp. 469–76.
3. One of the many texts influencing *Frankenstein* is Godwin's novel *St Leon: A Tale of the Sixteenth Century* (1799). Its protagonist, Reginald St. Leon, acquires both the philosopher's stone and the elixir of life. He achieves immortality but at the cost of alienation from other human beings.
4. The dark side of family life is explored in Shelley's 1819 novella, *Mathilda*, in which a father incestuously desires his daughter.
5. Lamb is a fascinating figure. Despite giving up poetry as a young man, and having little time for writing due to his job as a clerk for the East India Company, he produced some superb literary criticism and familiar essays, mainly for the *London Magazine* in the 1820s, and was on friendly terms with many of the major writers of his day. A good recent biography, which rightly emphasizes his close relationship with his sister, is Burton 2004.
6. For a more extended consideration for the relationship between *Frankenstein* and 'Alastor', particularly with regard to Orientalism, see Lew 1991, pp. 258–60.
7. For a full discussion of Hogg's and Hazlitt's representations of Shelley, see Higgins 2005, pp. 76–82.

CHAPTER 3: CONSTRUCTING A SELF: THE CREATURE'S NARRATIVE

1. Morton argues that the Creature is a very different sort of scientist from Frankenstein, a careful empiricist rather than a dangerous showman; see Morton 2002, pp. 145, 150. I take this point, but my view is that the novel tends to efface the distinction between the two categories.
2. Volney's full name is Constantin-Francois de Chasseboeuf, Comte de Volney and the full English title of the work is *The Ruins, or, Meditation on the Revolution of Empires*.
3. A brief but suggestive discussion of the relevance of particular 'lives' to the novel can be found in Shelley 1999, pp. 26–28.
4. See Lew 1991, pp. 278–83, for a discussion of this embedded narrative in the context of *Frankenstein*'s representation of 'the Orient'.
5. Various editors of the novel have pointed out that this scene alludes ironically to the passage in *Paradise Lost* where Eve is enchanted by her own reflection; see Milton (1968), IV, ll. 456–75. The allusion is discussed interestingly by Gilbert and Gubar 2000, pp. 240–41. The scene also alludes to the story of Narcissus falling in love with his own reflection in Ovid's *Metamorphoses* (Shelley 1996a, p. 85).

6. 'The Mirror Stage as Formative of the Function of the I as Revealed in Psychoanalytic Experience', in Lacan 2001, pp. 1–8. A sustained and suggestive Lacanian reading of *Frankenstein* by Peter Brooks can be found in Botting 1995a.
7. A brief discussion of Wollstonecraft's influence on *Frankenstein*, and some relevant extracts can be found in Shelley 1999, pp. 15–17, 254–63. In *Literature, Education, and Romanticism*, Alan Richardson argues that the description of the Creature's education follows Wollstonecraft's attack on 'the tradition of writing on female education and conduct [. . .] in which women are at once sentimentalized and viewed, anxiously, as deformed or monstrous in comparison with an explicitly male norm' (pp. 204–12).
8. For a Marxist reading of the novel which sees the Creature as symbolizing the working class, see the extract from Franco Moretti's *Signs Taken for Wonders* in Morton 2002, pp. 90–92.
9. It was reading Lipking's essay that first made me aware of the importance of this passage.

GUIDE TO FURTHER READING

PRIMARY TEXTS

Godwin, William (1998), *Caleb Williams*. Ed. David McCracken. Oxford: Oxford University Press. There are a number of parallels between this 1794 novel and *Frankenstein*, most notably in their treatment of loneliness, alienation and the law, and the doubling between the two protagonists.

Polidori, John William (2005), *'The Vampyre' and Other Writings*. Ed. Franklin Charles Bishop. Manchester: Carcanet. Contains three texts relevant to *Frankenstein*: 'The Vampyre', which Polidori based on Byron's 'A Fragment'; the novel *Ernestus Berchtold; or, the Modern Oedipus*; and extensive extracts from Polidori's diary for 1816.

Shelley, Mary (1999), *Frankenstein; or, the Modern Prometheus*. Ed. D. L. Macdonald and Kathleen Scherf. Ontario: Broadview. Based on the 1818 text, this edition's particular emphasis on the novel's intertextuality is reflected in the introduction and appendices of extracts from various authors, including Humphry Davy, William Godwin and Mary Wollstonecraft.

Shelley, Mary (2003), *Frankenstein or the Modern Prometheus*. Ed. Maurice Hindle. Harmondsworth: Penguin. This is based on the 1831 edition and contains a useful introduction.

Shelley, Mary (1994), *The Last Man*. Ed. Morton D. Paley. Oxford: Oxford University Press. In this novel, first published in 1826, and containing characters based on Byron and PBS, Shelley imagines the world in the twenty-first century beset by a terrible plague. It shares several themes with *Frankenstein*, including domesticity, politics, idealism and empire.

Shelley, Mary (2004), *Mathilda*. Ed. Janet Todd. Harmondsworth: Penguin. This tale of a father's incestuous desire for his daughter, written in 1819 but not published until 1959, offers a dark account of the bourgeois family that can be compared interestingly to *Frankenstein*. The Penguin edition prints it with two stories by Mary Wollstonecraft.

Shelley, Percy Bysshe (2002), *Shelley's Poetry and Prose*. Ed. Donald H. Reiman and Neil Fraistat. London: Norton. Apart from their intrinsic merit, several of PBS's poems are of interest as highly relevant to *Frankenstein*, including *Queen Mab*, *Alastor*, 'Hymn to Intellectual Beauty', 'Mont Blanc' and *Prometheus Unbound*.

SECONDARY TEXTS

Baldick, Chris (1990), *In 'Frankenstein''s Shadow: Myth, Monstrosity and Nineteenth-Century Writing*. Oxford: Oxford University Press. A fine study of the Frankenstein myth in nineteenth-century literature, which also has some intelligent things to say about the novel itself, particularly its relationship to the rhetoric of monstrosity surrounding the French Revolution.

Botting, Fred (1991), *Making Monstrous: 'Frankenstein', Criticism, Theory*. Manchester: Manchester University Press. A sophisticated post-structuralist analysis of the novel and critical approaches to it.

Botting, Fred (1995), *'Frankenstein'* [New Casebooks]. Basingstoke: Macmillan. A selection of ten important essays and extracts. Peter Brooks's 'What is a Monster? (According to *Frankenstein*)' is particularly recommended.

Botting, Fred (1995), *Gothic*. London: Routledge. An accessible and wide-ranging introduction to the genre.

Butler, Marilyn (1982), *Romantics, Rebels and Reactionaries*. Oxford: Oxford University Press. Probably still the best general study of British Romanticism.

Dart, Gregory (1999), *Rousseau, Robespierre and English Romanticism*. Cambridge: Cambridge University Press. An excellent study of Rousseau's impact on Romantic authors such as Mary Shelley, Godwin and Wollstonecraft, which pays particular attention to his autobiographical writings.

Fulford, Tim, Peter Kitson and Debbie Lee (2004), *Literature, Science and Exploration in the Romantic Era: Bodies of Knowledge*. Cambridge: Cambridge University Press. An important recent monograph that contains several chapters highly relevant to an understanding of *Frankenstein*.

Gilbert, Sandra M. and Gubar, Susan (2000; first published 1979), *The Madwoman in the Attic: The Woman Writer and the Nineteenth-Century Literary Imagination* (second edition). New Haven: Yale University Press. An enormously influential feminist study, which contains a fine chapter analysing *Frankenstein*'s troubled and complex engagement with *Paradise Lost*.

Jarvis, Robin (2004), *The Romantic Period: The Intellectual and Cultural Context of English Literature 1789–1830*. Harlow: Longman. A comprehensive and accessible study of the contexts of Romantic writing.

Levine, George and Knoepflmacher, U. C. (eds) (1979), *The Endurance of 'Frankenstein'*. Berkeley: University of California Press. A groundbreaking collection of essays covering a wide range of approaches to the novel. Those by Ellis, Griffin, Knoepflmacher, Levine and Sterrenburg are particularly stimulating.

Marshall, Tim (1995), *Murdering to Dissect: Graverobbing, 'Frankenstein', and the Anatomy Literature*. Manchester: Manchester University Press. An interdisciplinary study that places *Frankenstein* in the context of the discourses and legal framework surrounding the science of anatomy in the early nineteenth century.

McCalman, Iain (ed.) (1999), *An Oxford Companion to the Romantic Age*. Oxford: Oxford University Press. A very useful resource, combining short encyclopedia entries with essays on various aspects of Romantic-period history and culture.

Mellor, Anne K. (1989), *Mary Shelley: Her Life, Her Fiction, Her Monsters*. London: Routledge. An important feminist reading of Shelley's life and work, with a particular focus on *Frankenstein* and its contexts.

Morton, Timothy (ed.) (2002), *Mary Shelley's 'Frankenstein': A Sourcebook*. London: Routledge. A well-edited and useful collection of contextual material, critical interpretations and key passages from the novel.

Seymour, Miranda (2001), *Mary Shelley*. London: Picador. An evocative and readable recent biography.

ONLINE RESOURCES

Shelley, Mary Wollstonecraft. *Frankenstein; or, the Modern Prometheus: The Pennsylvania Electronic Edition*. Ed. Stuart Curran. University of Pennsylvania. <http://www.english. upenn.edu/Projects/knarf/frank.html>
This powerful resource includes indexes of characters and themes, and some useful contextual material.

Mary Wollstonecraft Shelley: Chronology and Resource Site. Ed. Shanon Lawson. June 1999. Romantic Circles. <http://www.rc. umd.edu/reference/chronologies/mschronology/mws.html>
Includes a reasonably detailed chronology of Shelley's life, and reproduces contemporary reviews of *Frankenstein* and *The Last Man*.

BIBLIOGRAPHY

PRIMARY TEXTS

Blake, William (2007), *The Complete Poems* (third edition). Ed. W. H. Stevenson. Harlow: Longman.

Burke, Edmund (1999), *The Portable Edmund Burke*. Ed. Isaac Kramnick. Harmondsworth: Penguin.

Byron, Lord George Gordon (2005), *Selected Poems*. Ed. Peter J. Manning and Susan J. Wolfson. Harmondsworth: Penguin.

Defoe, Daniel (2003), *Robinson Crusoe*. Ed. John Richetti. Harmondsworth: Penguin.

Goethe, Johann Wolfgang von (1989), *The Sorrows of Young Werther*. Trans. Michael Hulse. Harmondsworth: Penguin.

Godwin, William (1998), *Caleb Williams*. Ed. David McCracken. Oxford: Oxford University Press.

Godwin, William (2005), *St. Leon: A Tale of the Sixteenth Century*. Ed. William Brewer. Peterborough, Ontario: Broadview.

Hazlitt, William (1930–33), *The Complete Works of William Hazlitt*. Ed. P. P. Howe. 21 vols. London: J. M. Dent & Sons.

Lloyd, Charles and Lamb, Charles (1798), *Blank Verse*. London: John and Arthur Arch.

Locke, John (1993), *An Essay Concerning Human Understanding*. Ed. John W. Yolton. London: Everyman.

Milton, John (1968), *Paradise Lost*. Ed. Christopher Ricks. Harmondsworth: Penguin.

Mullan, John (ed.) (1996), *Lives of the Great Romantics*. 3 vols. London: William Pickering.

Polidori, John William (2005), *'The Vampyre' and Other Writings*. Ed. Franklin Charles Bishop. Manchester: Carcanet.

Rousseau, Jean-Jacques (1979a), *Émile or On Education*. Trans. Allan Bloom. New York: Basic Books.

Rousseau, Jean-Jacques (1979b), *Reveries of the Solitary Walker*. Trans. Peter France. Harmondsworth: Penguin.

Rousseau, Jean-Jacques (1984), *A Discourse on Inequality*. Trans. Maurice Cranston. Harmondsworth: Penguin.

Shelley, Mary (1987), *The Journals of Mary Shelley 1814–1844*. Ed. Paula R. Feldman and Diana Scott-Kilvert. 2 vols. Oxford: Clarendon Press.

Shelley, Mary (1992), *Frankenstein or the Modern Prometheus*. Ed. Maurice Hindle. Harmondsworth: Penguin.

Shelley, Mary (1994), *The Last Man*. Ed. Morton D. Paley. Oxford: Oxford University Press.

Shelley, Mary (1996a), 'Frankenstein: or the Modern Prometheus'. Ed. Nora Crook. In Volume 1. *The Novels and Selected Works of Mary Shelley*. 8 vols. London: Pickering and Chatto.

Shelley, Mary (1996b), *Frankenstein* [Norton Critical Edition]. Ed. John Paul Hunter. New York: Norton.

Shelley, Mary (1996c), *The 'Frankenstein' Notebooks*. Ed. Charles E. Robinson. New York: Garland.

Shelley, Mary (1998), *Frankenstein: or the Modern Prometheus. The 1818 Text*. Ed. Marilyn Butler. Oxford: Oxford University Press.

Shelley, Mary (1999), *Frankenstein; or, the Modern Prometheus*. Ed. D. L. Macdonald and Kathleen Scherf. Ontario: Broadview.

Shelley, Mary (2000), *Frankenstein* (second edition). Ed. Johanna M. Smith. Boston: Bedford/St Martin's.

Shelley, Mary (2004), *Mathilda*. Ed. Janet Todd. Harmondsworth: Penguin.

Shelley, Percy Bysshe (2002), *Shelley's Poetry and Prose*. Ed. Donald H. Reiman and Neil Fraistat. London: Norton.

Southey, Robert (1838), *Poetical Works*, 10 vols. London: Longman.

SECONDARY TEXTS

Baldick, Chris (1990), *In Frankenstein's Shadow: Myth, Monstrosity and Nineteenth-Century Writing*. Oxford: Oxford University Press.

Beck, Rudolf (2000), ' "The Region of Beauty and Delight": Walton's Polar Fantasies in Mary Shelley's *Frankenstein'*. *Keats-Shelley Journal*, 49, 24–29.

Behrendt, Stephen C., Ed. (1990), *Approaches to Teaching Shelley's 'Frankenstein'*. New York: Modern Language Association.

Botting, Fred (1991), *Making Monstrous: 'Frankenstein', Criticism, Theory*. Manchester: Manchester University Press.

Botting, Fred (ed.) (1995a), *'Frankenstein': Mary Shelley* [New Casebooks Series]. New York: St Martin's Press.

Botting, Fred (1995b), *Gothic*. London: Routledge.

Burton, Sarah (2004), *A Double Life: A Biography of Charles and Mary Lamb*. Harmondsworth: Penguin.

Butler, Marilyn (1982), *Romantics, Rebels and Reactionaries*. Oxford: Oxford University Press.

Cantor, Paul A. (1984), *Creature and Creator: Myth-making and English Romanticism*. Cambridge: Cambridge University Press.

Chantler, Ashley (1999), "The Waltons: *Frankenstein*'s Literary Family". *Byron Journal*, 27, 102–04.

Dart, Gregory (1999), *Rousseau, Robespierre and English Romanticism*. Cambridge: Cambridge University Press.

Docherty, Thomas (1983), *Reading (Absent) Character: Towards a Theory of Characterization in Fiction*. Oxford: Clarendon Press.

Favret, Mary A. (1993), *Romantic Correspondence: Women, Politics and the Fiction of Letters*. Cambridge: Cambridge University Press.

Feldman, Paula R. and Theresa M. Kelly (1995), *Romantic Women Writers: Voices and Countervoices*. Hanover, NH: University Press of New England.

Fulford, Tim, Peter Kitson and Debbie Lee (2004), *Literature, Science and Exploration in the Romantic Era: Bodies of Knowledge*. Cambridge: Cambridge University Press.

Gilbert, Sandra M. and Gubar, Susan (2000; first published 1979), *The Madwoman in the Attic: The Woman Writer and the Nineteenth-Century Literary Imagination* (second edition). New Haven: Yale University Press.

Greer, Germaine (2007), 'Arts Comment', *The Guardian*, 9 April, p. 28.

Heringman, Noah (2003), *Romantic Science: The Literary Forms of Natural History*. Albany: State University of New York Press.

Higgins, David (2005), *Romantic Genius and the Literary Magazine: Biography, Celebrity, Politics*. London: Routledge.

Holdsworth, Nadine and Luckhurst, Mary (eds) (2007), *A Concise Companion to British and Irish Drama*. London: Blackwell.

Jarvis, Robin (2004), *The Romantic Period: The Intellectual and Cultural Context of English Literature 1789–1830*. Harlow: Longman.

Lacan, Jacques (2001), *Écrits: A Selection*. Trans. Alan Sheridan. London: Routledge.

Leader, Zachary (1996), *Revision and Romantic Authorship*. Oxford: Oxford University Press.

Lee, Debbie (2002), *Slavery and the Romantic Imagination*. Philadelphia: University of Pennsylvania Press.

Levine, George and Knoepflmacher, U. C. (eds) (1979), *The Endurance of 'Frankenstein'*. Berkeley: University of California Press.

Lew, Joseph W. (1991), 'The Deceptive Other: Mary Shelley's Critique of Orientalism in *Frankenstein*'. *Studies in Romanticism*, 30, 255–83.

Malchow, H. L. (1993), 'Frankenstein's Monster and Images of Race in Nineteenth-Century Britain'. *Past and Present*, 139, 90–130.

Marshall, Tim (1995), *Murdering to Dissect: Graverobbing, 'Frankenstein', and the Anatomy Literature*. Manchester: Manchester University Press.

McCalman, Iain (ed.) (1999), *An Oxford Companion to the Romantic Age*. Oxford: Oxford University Press.

Mee, Jon (2003), *Romanticism, Enthusiasm, and Regulation: Poetics and the Policing of Culture in the Romantic Period*. Oxford: Oxford University Press.

Mellor, Anne K. (1989), *Mary Shelley: Her Life, Her Fiction, Her Monsters*. London: Routledge.

Morton, Timothy (ed.) (2002), *Mary Shelley's 'Frankenstein': A Sourcebook*. London: Routledge.

Newman, Beth (1986), 'Narratives of Seduction and the Seductions of Narrative: The Frame Structure of *Frankenstein*'. *English Literary History*, 53, 141–63.

O'Rourke, James (1989), ' "Nothing More Unnatural": Mary Shelley's Revision of Rousseau'. *English Literary History*, 56, 543–69.

Pollin, Burton R. (1965), 'Philosophical and Literary Sources of *Frankenstein*'. *Comparative Literature*, 17.2, 1965, 97–108.

Poovey, Mary (1980), 'My Hideous Progeny: Mary Shelley and the Feminization of Romanticism'. *PMLA*, 95.3, 332–47.

Randel, Fred V. (2003), 'The Political Geography of Horror in Mary Shelley's *Frankenstein*'. *English Literary History*, 70, 465–91.

Richard, Jessica (2003), ' "A Paradise of My Own Creation": *Frankenstein* and the Improbable Romance of Polar Exploration'. *Nineteenth-Century Contexts*, 25, 295–314.

Richardson, Alan (1994), *Literature, Education, and Romanticism: Reading as Social Practice, 1780–1832*. Cambridge: Cambridge University Press.

Rieger, James (1963), 'Dr Polidori and the Genesis of *Frankenstein*'. *Studies in English Literature 1500–1900*, 3.4, 461–72.

Ruston, Sharon (2005), *Shelley and Vitality*. Basingstoke: Palgrave Macmillan.

Taylor, Charles (1989), *Sources of the Self: The Making of Modern Identity*. Cambridge, MA: Harvard University Press.